MONKEY

Books by David Kherdian

Poetry

On the Death of My Father and Other Poems
Homage to Adana
Looking Over Hills
The Nonny Poems
I Remember Root River
The Farm
Taking the Soundings on Third Avenue
The Farm: Book Two
Place of Birth
Threads of Light
The Dividing River/The Meeting Shore

Novels

The Road From Home
It Started with Old Man Bean
Beyond Two Rivers
Finding Home
The Song in the Walnut Grove
The Mystery of the Diamond in the Wood
Bridger: The Story of a Mountain Man
A Song for Uncle Harry

Nonfiction

Six Poets of the San Francisco Renaissance
Root River Run (Memoir)
On a Spaceship with Beelzebub: By a Grandson of Gurdjieff

Translations

The Pearl: Hymn to the Robe of Glory
Pigs Never See the Stars: Proverbs from the Armenian
Monkey: A Journey to the West

MONKEY

A Journey to the West

DAVID KHERDIAN

*A retelling of the Chinese folk novel
by Wu Ch'eng-en*

SHAMBHALA
Boston & London
2000

Shambhala Publications, Inc.
Horticultural Hall
300 Massachusetts Avenue
Boston, MA 02115
www.shambhala.com

9 8 7 6 5 4 3
Printed in the United States of America
♾ This edition is printed on acid-free paper that meets the American
National Standards Institute Z39.48 Standard.

Distributed in the United States by Random House, Inc., and in Canada
by Random House of Canada Ltd

The illustrations presented with the text were selected from the 1833
Bunsei edition of *Journey to the West* and are reproduced courtesy of
the Harvard-Yenching Library, Harvard University.

Library of Congress Cataloging-in-Publication Data

Kherdian, David
    Monkey: a journey to the west/retold by David Kherdian.
    —1st ed.
        p.   cm.
    Based on Hsi yu chi/Wu Ch'eng-en.
    ISBN 1-57062-581-6
    1. Hsüan-tsang, 596 (ca.)–664—Fiction.   I. Wu, Ch'eng-en,
ca. 1500–ca. 1582. Hsi yu chi.   II. Title.   III. Title:
Journey to the west.
PS3561.H4M6   1992   91-50364
813'.54—dc20   CIP

Contents

Editor's Foreword   *vii*

1 Stone Monkey King   *1*

2 The Search for Immortality   *13*

3 Demon King of Havoc   *27*

4 Monkey's Iron Cudgel   *32*

5 A Messenger from Heaven   *41*

6 In the Cloud Palace of the Jade Emperor   *48*

7 Immortality Peaches and Golden Elixirs   *53*

8 Monkey Goes Too Far   *63*

9 In the Buddha's Palm   *74*

10 Kuan-yin's Search for a Pilgrim   *85*

11 The Journey to the West   *96*

12 Tripitaka Takes a Disciple   *106*

13 The Cap of Discipline   *116*

14 Riding the Dragon   *122*

15 Pigsy and the Dragon of the River
of Flowing Sands   *128*

16 Flaming Mountain and the Iron Fan   *143*

17 Fanning the Fire   *149*

18 The Bull Demon's Wife   *158*

19 Bull Demon Wins the Day   *172*

20 Putting Out the Fire   *178*

21 The Path Behind the Temple and
the Bottomless Boat   *189*

22 The Last Calamity   *195*

23 The Western Paradise   *203*

To Janwillem van de Wetering
for love of *Monkey*

Editor's Foreword

*P*ART historical epic and part social satire, the Chinese novel *Journey to the West* (*Hsi-yu-chi*), which also came to be known as *Monkey*, is probably the most popular book in all of East Asia. Thought to be written by Wu Ch'eng-en in the sixteenth century, *Journey to the West* was originally a massive work of one hundred chapters but was traditionally abridged to various lengths to suit different audiences. It is the story of the adventures of the rogue-trickster Monkey—and his encounters with a bizarre cast of demons, spirits, gods, and bodhisattvas—as he and his companions travel to India with the Buddhist pilgrim Hsüan-tsang, a historic figure of the seventh century.

Although the book is often described by Western translators as a folk novel, Chinese Buddhist, Taoist, and Confucian writers have all commented on its rich allegorical and symbolic content. One well-known eighteenth-century Taoist commentator, Liu I-ming, points out how *Journey to the West* "uses the theme of the journey to India to obtain Buddhist scriptures as a means of elucidating the secrets of the *Diamond Cutter* and *Lotus of the Truth*. It uses the theme of alchemy to open up the mysteries of the *Triplex Unity* and *Understanding Reality*. It uses the Chinese monk and his companions to expound the meanings of 'River' and 'Lo' diagrams and the *I Ching*." *Journey to the West*, Liu I-ming says, "explains both social realities and ultimate realities; it explains the times of nature and the affairs of humanity. When it comes to methods of learning Tao, self-cultivation, and dealing with society, *Journey to the West* explains them all."*

Even the most casual reader will notice the symbolic dimension of the novel. Its characters are archetypal figures representing universal qualities of human nature. Hsüantsang embodies "everyman," the ordinary and confused nature of all human beings. Pigsy symbolizes uncontrollable sensuality and pure appetite while also representing the vitality and energy necessary on the spiritual path. Less clear is the character Sandy, whom some Chinese commentators identify with the qualities of sincerity or wholeheartedness. And then, of course, there is Monkey, who epitomizes the restlessness of "monkey mind," which must be tamed by discipline before the spiritual journey can begin in earnest. The many demons and monsters encountered along the way can be seen as projections of the mind; once delusion is conquered these obstacles disappear and the goal is attained. Indeed, the entire journey can be seen as a spiritual allegory of the struggles of self-cultivation and the accumulation of merit on the spiritual path. Probably the most extraordinary quality of this classic is that it succeeds so wonderfully on both levels, as a profound allegory of the religious quest and as a picaresque adventure novel.

The story of Monkey is best known in the West through Arthur Waley's partial translation of *Journey to the West.*[†] Published in England in 1943, Waley's was the first attempt at a direct translation into English. Waley's version, however, tends to emphasize the text's literary rather than

---

* *Vitality, Energy, Spirit: A Taoist Sourcebook,* trans. Thomas Cleary (Boston: Shambhala Publications, 1991).

[†] Wu Ch'eng-en, *Monkey,* trans. Arthur Waley (New York: Grove Press, 1958).

spiritual dimension and skips over much of the original narrative (leaving out almost all of the second half of the journey), though the episodes that are included are presented in their entirety. David Kherdian's retelling, based on two complete translations of *Journey to the West*,* takes a somewhat more traditional approach, including many more of the original episodes, in an abbreviated form.

The illustrations in the interior and on the cover of this edition of *Monkey* have been drawn from a 1833 Japanese retelling of *Journey to the West*, illustrated by the famous woodblock artist Hokusai (1760–1849) and other artists.

---

* *The Journey to the West*, 4 vols., trans. and ed. Anthony C. Yu (Chicago: University of Chicago Press, 1977), and *The Journey to the West*, 4 vols., trans. W. J. F. Jenner (Beijing: Foreign Languages Press, 1982).

MONKEY

Stone Monkey King

*H*IGH atop a mountain, surrounded by favored earth that nourished magic fungi and wild orchids, there came to be a magic stone of immortal dimensions and properties. It was fructified by the seeds of Heaven and Earth, and by the essences of the sun and moon, until one day it was impregnated by divine inspiration, and became pregnant with a divine embryo. The embryo continued to develop in secret, until one day it burst open to reveal a stone egg. Once the egg was exposed to the elements, the wind soon transformed it into a stone monkey, complete in every way and in all aspects of its being.

With his first breath, Monkey began to run and climb, and as he bowed to the four quarters his steely eyes shot two beams of golden light toward the Palace of the Pole Star. Those twin shafts of light startled the Celestial Jade Emperor, who was sitting with his divine ministers in the Miraculous Mist of the Cloud Palace of Golden Arches. He immediately ordered Thousand-League Eye and Wind-Knowing Ears to open the Southern Gate of Heaven and look out.

The two captains hurried to the gate, and after looking with sharpened eyes and ever-keen ears, they returned to the Holy Chamber to make their report. "Your Majesty, the light you have seen comes from the borders of the country Ao-lai, east of the Exalted Continent, from the Mountain of Flowers and Fruit, where a magic stone gave birth to an egg that was transformed by the wind into a stone monkey who just now bowed to the four quarters, shooting beams of golden light toward the Palace of the Pole Star. But now he is eating, and the light is growing dim."

"It is nothing surprising," the Jade Emperor said. "These creatures from the world below are composed of the essences of Heaven and Earth, and therefore anything can happen."

Monkey was soon climbing trees and picking flowers and fruit, cavorting among the sandy hollows and building sand pagodas, chasing dragonflies and catching small lizards, tearing off creepers and weaving mats, and making new friends with tigers, wolves, leopards, and bears—and, of course, with apes and monkeys like himself.

All day long, Monkey and his cohorts played through the pine forest and washed themselves beside the green stream.

One morning all the monkeys followed the stream up to its source. It wasn't long before they came to a great waterfall. "Look! Look!" Monkey shouted. "A white rainbow arcing toward the heavens! A thousand strands of hurling waves, impenetrable by wind, their breath so cold it divides the green ranges! See how the noble cascade is suspended like a hanging curtain."

"Marvelous water, marvelous water," the monkeys chanted. "Why, it must travel all the way to the bottom of the mountain and extend as far as the sea!" After stretching their eyes to the edge of the horizon, they turned and said, "Why, if one among us could penetrate that curtain of water, discover its source, and return to us unharmed, we would make him our king."

"Yes! Yes!" they chanted, sending the challenge out again and again. Finally, after the third call, the stone monkey jumped forward and exclaimed, "I'll go!" Without another word, he crouched, screwed up his eyes, and leapt through the waterfall.

When Monkey opened his eyes again, to his great surprise he saw neither water nor waves, but a long, gleaming bridge. The only water to be seen came spilling under the long archway and flowed through a crack in the rock.

Walking toward the bridge, Monkey looked around at the magical scene. Through a glittering haze of mist and smoke he could see clouds like drifting jade that framed a quiet house with windows: flowers were growing over a marble bench, and dragon pearls hung in the archway. Multicolored flowers surrounded the entrance, and inside could be seen oval-shaped stone tables and chairs and beds, as well as stone pots and bowls and pans.

When Monkey arrived at the middle of the bridge, he noticed a stone tablet that read: "This Water Curtain Cave, in the Blessed Land of Flower Mountain, Leads to Heaven." Monkey was beside himself with joy. He crouched, squinted, and jumped back through the waterfall. "A great stroke of luck," he shouted, "a great stroke of luck!" All the other monkeys began screeching and jumping up and down. "What's it like on the other side?" they shouted. "How deep is the water?"

"No water at all," Monkey said. "There's an iron bridge, and off to one side a stone house . . ."

"But, but, but . . . ," sputtered the monkeys, "whatever do you mean? A stone house, a bridge, and no water?"

"It's all true," Monkey replied. "A stone house, with stone ovens, stone chairs and beds, stone couches and utensils. It has surely been sent from Heaven, and there is room there for all of us. It is called the Water Curtain Cave of the Blessed Land of Flower Mountain. Think of it, a retreat from the wind, with shelter from the rain, and no thunder and lightning. No frost or snow. The mist is warmed by a halo of holy light, and the pines are forever green, with rare flowers that blossom anew every day."

3

The Water Curtain Cave, in the Blessed Land of
Flower Mountain, Leading to Heaven

"Lead the way!" they shouted in unison. "Lead the way!"

Monkey jumped again to the other side, and at once called out, "Jump at once—hurry, hurry!" The boldest monkeys jumped immediately, but those who were timid stretched their necks this way and that and then drew them back, while they scratched their ears and rubbed their cheeks, all the while shrieking among themselves, until at last they jumped across in a single body.

They were all as puzzled as Monkey had been, and just as incredulous. But after they had crossed the bridge they entered the house, where they began at once to fight over the beds, hurling dishes about, dragging the couches from one room to another, and for all the world behaving just like monkeys, until at last they wore themselves out and fell in a heap upon the floor.

Monkey took a seat above them and raised his voice in a commanding tone. "A being is only as good as his word. Didn't you say that the one clever enough and brave enough to jump through the water curtain would be your king? Well then, I have done just that. And I found a cave heaven and put all of you in the position of good householders. What could be more enviable! What more could one want? Now you must bow to me as your king."

The monkeys immediately prostrated themselves before the stone monkey, after which they lined up in order of age to pay their homage. "Great King, forever our lord," they intoned, their paws pressed together in reverence.

At once outlawing the word *stone*, Monkey took the name Handsome Monkey King, and he quickly assigned cabinet posts to the various monkeys, gibbons, and baboons. Now that they were ensconced in Paradise, they spent their days roaming the Mountain of Flowers and Fruit; in the evenings they would return to the Water Curtain Cave. Keeping to themselves, never mingling with other beasts or birds, they went on living this way in perfect sympathy and accord.

Several hundred years went by in this fashion, until one day Monkey became depressed in the midst of a banquet and began to weep. "What is wrong, Your Majesty?" the monkeys asked, gathering about their king. "Why are you so sad?"

"I have just now been brooding over my future," Monkey replied. "What will be the outcome of me—of all of us— once our lives have been spent?"

"How can you think of such things!" the other monkeys exclaimed. "Do we not have daily banquets, here on this blessed mountain that provides for all our needs? We are neither under the rule of unicorns, nor are we controlled by the phoenixes."

"What you say is true," Monkey replied. "No human king can restrain us, nor are we terrorized by any bird or beast. But the day will come when I will grow old and weak, and Yama, the King of the Underworld of Death, will destroy my existence. What then will I have to look forward to, but to be born again on Earth, and to live again in vain?"

All the monkeys were suddenly brought face to face with the prospect of their own death; covering their faces, they began to weep. To everyone's surprise, a gibbon jumped up and exclaimed, "If this is what troubles Your Majesty, it proves you are inclined toward higher matters. Such thoughts as these must lead to enlightenment. Of the five divisions of living beings, only three are free of the King of Death."

"Do you know what they are?" Monkey asked.

"They are the buddhas, the immortals, and the holy sages. Only these are free of the wheel of reincarnation. They are as eternal as Heaven and Earth, as the mountains and rivers, as the sun and moon."

"Where are they to be found?" Monkey asked.

"In the human world," the gibbon replied, "in ancient caves, and on the holy mountains."

"In that case, I shall leave tomorrow and descend the mountain. If I have to wander to the corners of the Earth and to the edge of Heaven, I will find these immortals and learn their secret. In this way I will escape the clutches of King Yama and be free of the wheel of reincarnation."

Monkey traveled for nearly ten years, crossing continents and oceans, traveling by raft and by foot.

Monkey crossed the Eastern Ocean to the land of Jambudvipa, where he learned human ways and took on their dress and manners. He wandered through the Eastern Continent for several years, but everywhere he went he saw the same thing: people preoccupied with fame and fortune, none giving a thought to the end that awaited each and every one of them. After traveling from city to city, he came at last to the Western Ocean. Surely, he thought, immortals must reside somewhere beyond this place.

Having crossed the Western Ocean, he came to the Western Continent, where he could see in the distance a great mountain. After he had climbed halfway up the eastern slope, he heard, to his great surprise, a human voice reciting a song.

> Happy and without woes of any kind,
> With ax in hand along my simple way,
> Singing through the marketplace,
> I barter wood for three pints of rice.
> Free of scheming and plotting and with
> Simplicity my life's intention,

I meet immortals everywhere I go
Expounding the Yellow Court.

"At last I have found the immortals," Monkey thought.
But when he leaped out of the woods he was startled to find an
ordinary-looking woodsman cutting branches from a dead
tree. Monkey braced himself and said, "Old immortal, your
disciple stands before you."

The woodsman dropped his ax in astonishment. "Why
do you address me as an immortal? I am nothing but a poor,
hungry woodcutter."

"If you are not an immortal, why do you talk like one?"

"What have I said to give you such an idea?"

"When I came to the edge of the woods I heard you
singing, 'I meet immortals everywhere I go, expounding the
Yellow Court.' The Yellow Court is a secret Taoist text, anyone who would utter those words must be an immortal."

"Anything but," sputtered the woodsman, "anything
but! However, I must tell you that my neighbor is an immortal, and it is he who taught me that verse. He gave me this song
to sing to lighten my cares, for he knows how hard I work and
how little I earn. I was anxious just now and so I sang my song.
It never occurred to me that I would be overheard."

"But if the immortal lives close by, why don't you become his disciple and learn the formula of eternal youth?"

"I've had a hard life," the woodsman answered. "My
father died when I was still a boy, and my mother remained a
widow. Since I have no brothers or sisters, the care of my
mother, who is now aged, fell to me. Our land is unfit for
farming, and so there is nothing for me to do but to cut
bundles of firewood in exchange for a few pennies with which
to buy our rice and tea. As you can see, I have no time for
austerities and magic."

"From what you say I can see that you are a devoted son, and I am sure your piety will be rewarded one day. I ask no more of you than to show me where the immortal lives, for I am in search of the Way."

"He lives not far from here," the woodcutter said. "The mountain we are on is called Mind Heart Mountain, and the immortal you seek lives in the Cave of the Slanting Moon and Three Stars. His name is Patriarch Subodhi. He has produced his share of disciples, and at the moment he has thirty or forty students. If you will take this narrow path before us you will come to his cave, just two or three miles from here."

Monkey found the cave without any trouble, but as the door was tightly shut he was afraid to knock. Instead, he jumped into a pine tree and began eating seeds and jumping about from branch to branch. Suddenly the door creaked open and a young boy stepped out of the dark chamber entrance. Monkey was instantly aware that this was no ordinary boy. He could tell from his impeccable dress and outward calm that he was a disciple of the immortal. The boy did not see Monkey in the tree and called out, "Who is making all the commotion?"

Monkey scrambled down from the tree and bowed to the boy. "I have come to study with the Patriarch. The last thing I would wish to do is to make a disturbance."

The boy looked Monkey up and down and smiled to himself. "So you are a seeker on the Way. My master is about to give a lecture, but before announcing the theme he asked me to check at the door to see if anyone had come along seeking instruction. I suppose he meant you."

"Of course he meant me," Monkey said, suddenly emboldened.

"Come with me, then," the boy replied.

Monkey brushed the dust from his sleeves and straightened his trousers before following the boy into the secret chambers of the cave. They passed row upon row of lofty towers, with huge alcoves containing cloisters and retreats, followed by meditation chambers and contemplative cells. At last they came to a green jade platform, where the Patriarch Subodhi was solemnly seated, with thirty-six lesser immortals assembled beneath him.

Monkey approached without hesitation and, kowtowing before the Master, began to bang his head against the floor, saying, "Master, Master, my deepest obeisance."

"Where are you from?" the Patriarch asked. "Tell me your country and name before paying further respects."

"I come from the Water Curtain Cave, of the Flower Mountain, in the country of Ao-lai."

"Get rid of him," the Patriarch roared. "He is full of duplicity and mischief. Even with right conduct he could not get anywhere."

"I am telling the truth!" Monkey exclaimed, banging his head once more against the floor. "I beseech you to believe me."

"If you are telling the truth, then how can you say you come from the country of Ao-lai? We are separated by two oceans and the Southern Continent."

"For ten years and more I have been traveling in search of the teaching. I have crossed oceans, wandered over frontiers, and traveled across many lands."

"So you have come by stages. Very well, then. Now tell me of your family."

"I have no family," Monkey replied.

"Then you must have been born in a tree."

"Not exactly," Monkey answered. "I came out of a magic stone. When the time was right, it burst open and there I was."

*The Taoist Patriarch Subodhi, in the Cave of
the Slanting Moon and Three Stars at Mind Heart Mountain*

"I see," the Patriarch said, for he was pleased. "In other words, you were born of Heaven and Earth. Now stand up and walk around so I can see all sides of you. I will need to give you a name. There is a word I use for each division and year of my teaching, which consists of twelve words in all."

"What are the twelve words?" Monkey asked.

"They are Wide, Great, Wise, Sharp, True, Conforming, Nature, Ocean, Quick, Aware, Complete, Awakened. Since you fall in the tenth generation of my teaching, your name must include the word *aware*. Your religious name, therefore, will be Aware-of-Vacuity."

"Marvelous!" Monkey exclaimed, clapping his hands, "from now on I will be called Aware-of-Vacuity."

$$\sim 2 \sim$$

The Search for Immortality

*F*OR his first lesson Monkey was taught deportment: how to ask questions properly and with courtesy, how to sit and stand and go through doors. His daily routine consisted of the study of language and etiquette, scriptures and doctrine; in addition to discussions of the Way, he practiced writing calligraphy and burning incense. During breaks in his study, Monkey would sweep the grounds and hoe the garden, where he assisted in planting flowers and pruning trees. He also gathered firewood, lit fires, fetched water, and served drinks. With all his needs provided for, and with his days occupied in study and chores, the years slipped by.

One day the Patriarch, while seated on his dais, began a lecture on the Way. Monkey sat entranced. It was as if jewels were falling from the Patriarch's mouth, echoing like thunder and shaking the Nine Heavens, revealing to each disciple the understanding of his true nature, and how to avoid the wheel of recurrence. Agitated with delight, Monkey began pulling at his ears and rubbing his cheeks. He was soon waving his arms and stamping his feet.

Suddenly the Patriarch fell silent; then, looking down at Monkey and fixing him with his gaze, he shouted, "What's the sense of your being here, when instead of listening you jump up and down like a madman?"

"I couldn't help myself," Monkey answered. "What you said brought such joy to my heart that I couldn't control my emotions. Please forgive me."

"So you have comprehended the true spirit of the Way. Tell me how long you have been with us."

"I have not counted the time, Master. I only know that in getting firewood I sometimes find myself in a grove of peach trees. I have had my fill of those peaches seven times."

"The slope where those peaches are found is called Succulent Peach Hill. If you have eaten of those peaches seven times, it must mean that you have been here seven years. What method of the Way would you like to learn from me?"

"That's up to you," Monkey said.

"There are three hundred and sixty divisions," the Patriarch said, "and all of them lead to illumination. Which division would you like to follow?"

"Whichever you think best," Monkey said. "I am your obedient pupil."

"How about the Magic Arts?" the Patriarch asked. "Would you like me to teach you that?"

"Of what do the Magic Arts consist?" Monkey asked.

"They consist of summoning the immortals and rising with the phoenix, shuffling yarrow sticks, pursuing good fortune and avoiding evil."

"Does this way lead to immortality?"

"Impossible," the Patriarch replied.

"Then it's not for me," Monkey said.

"In that case, how would you like to learn the Way of the Ways?"

"How does that go?"

"Why, it means studying the methods of Confucius, the Buddha, the Tao, the Dualists, the Mohists, and the Physicians, as well as chanting and reciting prayers. You will be able to conjure up saints and priests and suchlike."

"And will I be able to live forever?"

"Of course not!" the Patriarch shouted. "The Way of the Ways is no better than a pillar inside a wall."

"Master, I am a simple fellow," Monkey declared. "Skip the jargon and tell me what you mean."

"A pillar in this instance represents a main support in the building of a house, but one day the house falls into ruin, the pillar rots, and everything collapses."

"Doesn't sound like life unending to me," Monkey exclaimed. "Let's skip it."

"How about the Way of Silence, then?" the Patriarch said. "In the Way of Silence we must refrain from eating meat products. There is also fasting, walking, sitting and standing meditation, restraint, inactivity, quiescence, trance states, and, finally, being immured in a self-imposed wall of silence."

"Can all these activities and inactivities bring about immortality?" Monkey asked.

"The results of such quietism," the Patriarch said, "are no better than unfired clay in a kiln."

"You're getting technical again," Monkey said. "You'll have to keep it simple if you want Monkey to understand."

"It is not enough to shape the clay," the Patriarch said. "The elements of earth and water must be fired, or one day the rains will come and the clay will crumble and dissolve."

"No future in that," Monkey said. "Not interested."

"How would you like to learn the Way of Action?" the Patriarch asked.

"What are the activities in the Way of Action?"

"Well," the Patriarch began, "gathering the ying and soothing the yang, drawing the bow and driving the arrow, and rubbing the navel to assist the subtle flow of life, are some of the ways. There are also alchemical practices, which involve burning bushes and forging cauldrons, taking Red Mercury, purifying Autumn Stone, drinking Bride's Milk, and other such things.''

"Would I then live forever?"

"It would be as possible to live forever from doing such things as it would be to fish the moon out of a pool of water.''

"There you go again talking mumbo jumbo. I told you I'm a simpleton and can't make head or tail of this kind of talk.''

"It simply means,'' the Patriarch said, growing impatient, "that the moon is in the sky, only its reflection is in the water. To believe the moon can be scooped from water is to suffer from illusion.''

"In other words, nothing. Skip it! Skip it! Not interested.''

The Patriarch leapt from the dais and, pointing at Monkey with his ruler, cried, "You execrable ape! You won't learn this and you won't learn that, so what good is your being here?'' He struck Monkey three times on the head and marched out of the room with his arms folded behind his back. Turning briefly to dismiss all his pupils, he then locked the door behind him.

The moment he was out of sight all the other disciples turned on Monkey. "You miserable ape!'' they shouted. "You ungrateful, unmannerly, unteachable blockhead! The Master was willing to teach you anything you liked—what an opportunity!—but instead you find fault with this and find fault with that, until you have finally exasperated the Patriarch, and now we don't know when we'll see him again.''

But even as Monkey was being berated he felt an inward joy, because he knew something none of the other disciples knew. He might not have understood the jargon of the Way, but he understood the language of secret signs. When the Master had aimed three blows at Monkey's head, he was giving him an appointment at the third watch, and by folding his arms behind his back and then locking the door, he meant that Monkey was to come in by the back door, where he would receive the Master's instruction in secret.

Monkey spent the rest of the afternoon together with the other disciples in front of the cave, but while the others frolicked, he impatiently waited for evening to fall. After retiring with the others, Monkey waited for everyone to fall asleep. Since there are no guardians in the mountains to beat out the watch and call the hours, there was no ordinary way for Monkey to learn the time, but by calculating his breath with each inhalation and exhalation he was able to determine the hour of the Rat. Quietly he rose from his pallet, slipped into his clothes, and tiptoed out of the cave.

The moon shone brightly on the clear, cool dew. In the stillness the gurgling brook could be heard in the glen. Fireflies glowed in the gathering dark, while wings of the columned geese beat through the clouds. It was the precise hour of the third watch: time to seek the Perfect Way of Truth.

Monkey found the rear door of the Patriarch's chamber ajar. He slipped quietly inside and made his way into the inner chamber. The Master lay on his bed, facing the wall, with his body curled up in a posture of sleep. Monkey knelt beside the bed and waited. Presently the Patriarch awoke and began murmuring to himself.

Hard! Hard! Hard!
The Way is most obscure.
The Golden Elixir must be secret and sacred.
To teach the dark mysteries to the imperfect man
Is to confound the jaw, confuse the tongue,
And tire the brain.

Monkey collected himself, took a deep breath, and spoke. "Master, I've been kneeling here for some time, waiting for you to instruct me in the way of immortal life."

The Patriarch sat bolt upright. Turning sharply, he drew his legs underneath him and sat facing his intruder. "Audacious Monkey!" he exclaimed. "What are you doing in my chambers? Why aren't you with the other disciples?"

"After you spoke to us today," Monkey said, "I understood you to tell me that I was to come to you at the third watch, by way of the rear entrance, in order to receive your instructions in private."

The Patriarch was very pleased and could not conceal his smile. He thought to himself, "This wretched monkey must surely be the product of Heaven and Earth. How else could he have read my signs?"

"We are all alone," Monkey said. "Take pity on your humble disciple and teach me the way of immortality."

"It is clear that you are one who has been predestined," the Patriarch said. "Come close and listen carefully, and I will reveal to you the secret of long life."

Monkey was beside himself. He beat his head on the floor in gratitude, cleaned out his ears, and leaned forward in a kneeling position.

The Patriarch recited:

> This is the formula, sacred and true,
> Tend and spare the vital forces, this alone you
>   must do.
> In spirit, essence, and breath, the sacred powers
>   reside,
> Guard and protect these, let no others be aware.
> Keep to the Way, and the Way will keep you still.
> Learn the formulas, remember the spells,

Moon holds Jade Rabbit, the sun a Golden Crow,
Tortoise and Snake tightly held forever in secret
    embrace.
Tightly intertwined, the inner and outer forces
    grow strong.
Grasp the Five Elements, transpose, transform,
    transcend.
When this has been attained, you will Be—
Whether buddha or immortal, it is up to you.

Monkey was overcome. The teaching had reached to his inner core. He had carefully memorized the Patriarch's words, possessing the formula and divining the spell.

Three years passed as swiftly as a storm-driven cloud. Once again the disciples were gathered around their Patriarch, who was discoursing on parables and scholastic deliberations. Suddenly he cast his eyes down and asked, "Where is the disciple Aware-of-Vacuity?"

Monkey came forward and, after kowtowing, knelt before the Patriarch. "What has been the result of your stay with us?" the Patriarch asked. "Tell me which of the arts you have been practicing lately."

"The foundation of my understanding has grown," Monkey said, "and I am beginning to see the One in the All."

"If you have apprehended the dharma-nature, and have seen the origin of things, then you have entered within the divine substance. You must therefore be aware of the Three Calamities."

"There must be some mistake," Monkey rejoined. "Isn't it true that once the Way has been mastered, one might live forever, free of illness and protected from fire and water? What do you mean by the Three Calamities?"

"You have mixed the elixir and defied the gods and demons, invading the dark mysteries of the sun and moon," said the Patriarch. "Although you may keep your youthful appearance and have extended the length of your life, after five hundred years Heaven will send down the Calamity of Thunder and strike you on the spot unless you have found the way to protect yourself ahead of time. If you succeed in avoiding it, your age will indeed approach that of Heaven, otherwise you will be struck dead.

"After another five hundred years," the Patriarch continued, "Heaven will send down the Calamity of Fire to destroy you. This is no common fire but, being hidden, rises up through the soles of your feet to the top of your head, reducing your limbs and organs to ashes, and your one thousand years of self-perfecting will have been a waste of time.

"If you escape this calamity, in another five hundred years the Calamity of Wind will come. It is not the wind of the east, south, west, or north, nor of the four seasons. It is neither the Flower Wind, or the Willow Wind, or the Pine or Bamboo Wind. It is the Monster Wind. It enters through the skull, down through the six entrails and nine orifices, until your bones dissolve and your body disintegrates.

"You must avoid each of these Three Calamities if you are to be immortal."

Monkey's hair stood on end. He kowtowed reverently until at last he was able to collect himself and speak. "I implore you, Master, teach me the remedies to ward off the disaster of the Three Calamities, and I will always be in your debt."

"That would not be difficult," the Patriarch said, "if it weren't for your peculiarities."

Monkey objected, "I have a round head pointing to the Heavens, and square feet for stomping over the earth. Similarly, I have nine orifices and four limbs, organs and entrails and cavities. How am I different from other people?"

"It is true, in many ways you are just the same, but you have much less jowl. Further, you have sunken cheeks and a pointy chin."

"The Master doesn't see that I provide my own balance. If I have less cheek, then I have more paunch."

For some reason, the Patriarch was mollified. "Very well, then," he said, "there are but two methods of escape. You must decide which one you would like to learn. There is the Art of the Heavenly Ladle, which numbers thirty-six transformations, and there is the Art of the Earthly Multitude, which numbers seventy-two transformations."

"Seventy-two!" Monkey shouted. "If everything else is equal, I'll take the Art of the Earthly Multitude."

"Step forward, then," the Patriarch said, "and I will whisper the formula in your ear."

Now, Monkey was no ordinary mortal. Because he had long ago trained himself to do one thing well, he could now perfect anything he set his mind to. He immediately memorized the oral formulas, and by practicing them in secret he soon mastered all seventy-two transformations.

One day the Patriarch and a number of his pupils were admiring the evening view in front of Three Stars Cave. The Master turned to Monkey and asked, "How are you getting along with the special work I gave you?"

"Thanks to your kindness, Master, I have attained near-perfection. I am already able to soar above the clouds."

"Let us see you fly," the Patriarch commanded.

Monkey put his feet together and somersaulted more than fifty feet into the air; after walking over the clouds for several miles, he dropped down in front of the Patriarch. Folding his arms across his chest, he said, "Master, that's what I call flying and soaring in the clouds."

The Patriarch laughed. "I don't call that cloud-soaring, I call that cloud-crawling. We have a saying, 'The immortal travels to the Northern Ocean in the morning, and by evening is in Ts'ang-wu.' "

"What is meant by that saying?" Monkey asked.

"Real cloud-soarers start from the Northern Ocean in the morning, and from there they journey through the Eastern Ocean, the Western Ocean, the Southern Ocean, and then return to Ts'ang-wu, which is another name for Ling-ling in the Northern Ocean. To travel all four seas in one day, that's true cloud-soaring."

"Sounds difficult," Monkey said.

"Nothing in this world is difficult, but thinking makes it seem so. Where there is true will, there is always a way."

"Master, you may as well complete the work you started. Please be so kind as to teach me true cloud-soaring. I will remain forever grateful."

The Patriarch said, "When true immortals want to soar to the clouds, they merely stamp their feet and rise straight up from that position. I noticed that you had to pull yourself up by jumping. I will teach you the cloud somersault in accordance with your form."

Monkey kowtowed before the Patriarch, who bent over and whispered the magic formula in his ear. "Now," the Patriarch said, straightening himself, "you must make the magic pass, recite the spell, clench your fists tightly, shake yourself, and with one somersault you will be able to fly 108,000 miles."

When the others heard about this they said, "Lucky Monkey! Lucky Monkey! If he can learn this trick he can become a sky courier, and by delivering official letters and reports he'll always be able to make a living."

By now it was dark, and the Master and his disciples went back to their quarters. But Monkey practiced throughout the night until he had perfected the cloud trapeze. Now at last he had achieved immortality and perfect bliss.

One day early in the summer the disciples, having taken a break from their work, were gathered at the edge of the pine forest, discussing the Way and its methods among themselves. They turned to Monkey and asked, "What did you do in a former incarnation to merit the formula for avoiding the Three Calamities? Have you mastered all the exercises and transformations the Master gave you?"

"It goes without saying that I am indebted to the Master," Monkey said, "but it is also true that I have worked day and night to perfect myself. There isn't a single transformation I have not mastered."

"What better time for a demonstration?" they said. "How about showing us?"

This was all the encouragement Monkey needed, for he was more than willing to display his magic powers. "What kind of transformation would you like to see?" he asked.

"Turn yourself into a pine tree," one of them said. Monkey made the magic pass, recited the spell, clenched his fists, shook himself, and changed into a pine tree.

The disciples looked at the tree in amazement. It was a pine tree, to be sure, but straighter, truer, and higher than all the others, with a nobility of bearing that was unmistakable. They began to cheer and clap their hands. "Bravo! Bravo! Marvelous Monkey!" they cried.

悟空化 ごくうのへんげ
大松驚 たいしょうおどろく
衆人 もろもろのひと

The Taoist disciples look on in amazement as Monkey transforms himself into a pine tree.

The Patriarch heard the uproar and came charging in their direction, staff in hand. "Who is causing all this racket!" he bellowed. The disciples quickly recovered themselves and, standing meekly before their Master, began stuttering so that they were unable to complete a word among themselves. Monkey quickly resumed his true form and shouted from the woods, "There is no one here but us, Master. We were having a heated discussion, that is all."

"I heard yelling and screaming. This is no way for those who are cultivating right conduct to behave. Don't you know by now that when you open your mouths the vital forces dissipate, and that the wagging of tongues always leads to trouble?"

The disciples had never seen their Master this angry. They were so frightened that they confessed to the truth at once. "Monkey did a transformation for us. We asked him to change into a pine tree and he did it so perfectly that we couldn't help but applaud. We beg your forgiveness."

"Go away, all of you! All except Monkey." When the others had left and Monkey stepped forward, the Patriarch asked, "Is this the way you use your spiritual powers? Turning into—what was it—a pine tree? Do you suppose I taught you those transformations so you could show off? Don't you realize that by turning tricks you will encourage others to wish to do the same? And have you considered what will happen if you withhold your secrets? Why, they will punish you! Thanks to your wickedness you have put yourself in grave danger."

"Please forgive me," Monkey pleaded.

"I won't punish you," the Patriarch said, "but you can no longer stay here."

Monkey began to cry. "Where am I to go?"

"Back where you came from, I suppose."

"Do you mean that I should return to the Water Curtain Cave on the Mountain of Flowers and Fruit, in the country of Ao-lai?"

"Why not?" the Patriarch said. "If you return at once you will be able to preserve your life. One thing is certain, you cannot stay here."

"Although I have not thought of home in all the twenty years I have been away, to tell you the truth I now find that there is something in me that longs to return. But how can I depart from my Master without repaying his many kindnesses to me?"

"Your leaving is kindness enough. Just see to it that any troubles you get into do not reflect on me. That is all I ask in the way of kindness from you. Now be off!"

Monkey could see there was no use in arguing. After taking leave of the other disciples, he came before his Master and bowed one final time. The Patriarch remained unbending. "I am convinced that no good will come of you. The trouble you are bound to cause I can do nothing about, but I forbid you ever to say that you have been my disciple. If you utter my name even once I will know of it, and I assure you I will skin you alive, break all your bones, and banish your soul to the Place of Ninefold Darkness, from where it will not be released for ten thousand aeons."

"I'll not utter a single letter of your name," Monkey said. "I will say that I learned everything by myself." Thanking the Patriarch one last time, Monkey turned, made the magic pass, and rode off on a cloud to the Eastern Ocean.

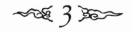

Demon King of Havoc

*I*T took Monkey less than an hour to reach the Mountain of Flowers and Fruit. He lowered his cloud and began to hear in the distance the call of cranes and the cries of monkeys. "Little ones," he called out, "I have returned."

From the crannies in the cliffs, from the woods and out of the trees, from among the flowers and the bushes, monkeys large and small by the tens of thousands came rushing forward to meet Handsome Monkey King. They kowtowed all around him, shouting, "Long live the Monkey King!" When they had calmed down, one of the gibbons asked, "Why did you abandon us for such a long time? We have been desperate without you. For some time now we have been brutally abused by a monster who has robbed us of our possessions and taken over our Water Cave, whence he has carried many of our children. You have returned just in time. In another year we would have lost everything in our mountain home: our cave, our children—everything!"

Monkey became furious. "Who is this lawless monster who has invaded our territory and outraged my subjects?"

"Your Majesty, he calls himself the Demon King of Havoc, and he lives north of here. That is all we know. He comes like a cloud and leaves like the mist, as unpredictable as the wind and the rain, the thunder and the lightning. We have no idea where he lives."

"In that case," Monkey said, "go on with your games, and don't be afraid. I will go and find him myself." Monkey leaped into the air and somersaulted toward the north. It wasn't long before he came to a tall, rugged mountain. Upon landing he began to look about, when he heard voices in the distance. Scrambling down the slope, he came to the Water Belly Cave at the foot of a cliff. At the entrance of the cave several imps were frolicking and singing.

"Stop!" Monkey shouted. "I am the King of the Water Curtain Cave. Go tell your master—the Demon King of Havoc, or whatever he is called—that I've come back to square matters with him. He has been mistreating my little ones, and now he must answer to me."

The imps scurried into the cave, shouting, "Great King, a disastrous thing has happened!"

"What disaster?" the Demon roared.

"A monkey creature is standing just outside the cave who claims to be the lord of the Water Curtain Cave, and he says you have been ill-treating his subjects. He's come to settle matters with you."

The Demon roared with laughter. "So," he said, "the king they speak about who went away to practice the arts of the Way really exists. Tell me how he is dressed and what weapons he is carrying."

"He has no weapons," they said. "He is bare-headed and is dressed in a red robe with a yellow sash, and a pair of black boots. He doesn't have the appearance of an ordinary citizen, nor does he look like a monk. And he doesn't appear to be a Taoist or an immortal, either. He is making his demands with empty hands and bare fists."

"Bring me my armor and weapons," the Demon commanded. The imps hurried away and soon returned with the Demon's paraphernalia, whereupon he adjusted his breastplate and helmet, grasped his sword and marched out of the cave, his followers trailing behind him. "Where is the King of the Water Curtain Cave? Speak up!'' Because the Demon had been expecting a monster like himself, he did not even see his adversary.

"You reckless and insolent wretch," Monkey said. "Don't tell me you can't see Old Monkey!"

The Demon looked down with derision and spat on the ground. "Why, you're barely four feet tall, and you are still a youngster. What kind of fool are you to challenge me without weapons or any means of defense? How dare you talk of settling accounts with me!"

"Don't believe your eyes," Monkey said. "You say I am small, but I can make myself as tall as I please. You claim I am unarmed, but with these hands I could tear the moon out of the sky. Hold still, and we will see how you like the taste of Monkey's fists." Leaping into the air, Monkey aimed a blow at the Demon's face. Parrying the blow with his hand, the Demon said, "A dwarf like you is no challenge to a warrior like me. I won't shame myself by using a sword on the likes of you."

"Well said," Monkey cried, "but your boasting is short-lived." The Demon twirled and struck, but Monkey dodged the blow and closed in on him. They began flying around, kicking and pummeling each other. Monkey had a clear advantage, with his short blows finding their mark more often than did the wild strikes of the long-armed Demon.

The Demon seized his sword and came after Monkey. Monkey dodged the first blow, but then, seeing that the Demon had become ferocious, he employed the technique of Body Outside the Body. Plucking several hairs from his body, he popped them into his mouth and began to chew them into tiny bits. Then, spitting them into the air, he cried, "Change!" Monkey's bits of hair were immediately transformed into several hundred monkeys. They swarmed around the Demon, skipping over him and pulling at his clothes, and kicked and punched him, pinching his nose and poking at his eyes. They were so nimble that no sword or spear could touch them.

The Demon was so agitated that he dropped his sword and began using his spear like a cudgel. Now Monkey swooped down and found the Demon's sword lying on the ground. Pushing back through the throng of little monkeys, he raised the sword and brought it down on the Demon's head with such force that the monster's skull split in two.

With his charges following at his heel, Monkey then rushed back into the cave and together they made quick work of the imps. By reciting the magic spell, Monkey called back his hairs. As he looked around at the monkeys still present, he realized that these were the ones the Demon had carried off from the Water Curtain Cave.

Monkey next set fire to the Water Belly Cave, reducing it to ashes. Then he took his little ones home on his cloud trapeze. The following day a great banquet was prepared in honor of Monkey's return, and also to celebrate the destruction of the Demon King of Havoc. After the festivities all the monkeys gathered around their king and sang his praises. "We had no idea when you left us," they said, "that you would be able to acquire such magic arts. Please tell us, Your Majesty, how you came to possess such powers."

"When I left you," Monkey began, "I went across the Eastern Ocean to the land of Jambudvipa, where I learned human ways. I swaggered about for eight or nine years in this fashion with very little purpose, and drew no closer to enlightenment. Nor did I have any luck in finding the Way. Then I crossed the great Western Ocean, where in time I was fortunate enough to find an old Patriarch who taught me the secret of eternal life."

One of the wise old monkeys said, "Such luck is not to be met with even after ten thousand turns of the wheel of life."

"Yes! Yes!" the others chanted. "Not to be met with in ten thousand turns. Hail our protector, the Handsome Monkey King!"

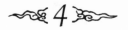

Monkey's Iron Cudgel

*M*ONKEY had returned to his kingdom in triumph. Using the cutlass with which he had slayed the Demon, he began to practice swordplay every day, while he taught the little monkeys the arts of war. They began sharpening bamboo spears and making swords out of wood. Using their weapons, they went on patrol, learned to advance and retreat, pitched camp, and built stockades. And in this manner the days went by.

One day Monkey grew very quiet, and sitting by himself he began to muse aloud. "These games we are now playing may have a real counterpart. What if the time came that we were invaded? Suppose our whereabouts became known and a human monarch or even some beast or bird king took the notion that we were hatching a plot against his kingdom and decided to invade our country and attack us. What good then would be our bamboo spears and wooden swords? We must have proper cutlasses and halberds, but where are such things to be found?"

Four old monkeys came forward and arranged themselves before their King, kowtowing respectfully. A gibbon was the first to speak. "Your Majesty, if it is real weapons you are seeking, nothing could be easier."

"How can that be?" Monkey asked.

"At the frontier of Ao-lai, east of our mountain and across two hundred miles of water, dwells a king with a large standing army. He is bound to have weapons of every kind.

They will certainly either sell you weapons or make what you need. Once we have been trained with real weapons, no one will be able to invade us, and we will be able to live without fear."

Monkey was delighted. "Stay here and take care of yourselves," he said, "and I will go and see what I can accomplish."

Sailing off on his cloud trapeze, Monkey soon came to a walled city with a circular moat, broad avenues, marketplaces, and human dwellings in the thousands. People were walking about under the sun, seemingly without a care in the world. "I have come to the right place," Monkey thought. "I can either go down and buy what I need or, better yet, acquire whatever I want by magic." Making a sign and reciting a spell, he faced the southeast and, drawing in his breath, blew forth a gale. The king and all his subjects were so alarmed they bolted their gates, doors, and windows.

Monkey lowered his cloud and came sailing in past the Imperial Gate, to the door of the armory. When he forced the door open and stared inside, he could scarcely believe his eyes. There before him, in room upon room, were weapons of every kind and description: scimitars, spears, swords, halberds, battle-axes, scythes, whips, rakes, drums and drumsticks, bows and crossbows, arrows, forks, lances, cudgels, pikes, maces, tridents, and clubs. "How many of these can I possibly carry by myself?" Monkey pondered. "I'd better use my Body-out-of-Body magic." He plucked several hairs from his body and, after chewing them into bits, spat them into the air, saying, "Change!" The armory was suddenly filled with chattering monkeys. At once they began to collect the weapons, each according to his size and strength, until they had plundered the entire arsenal. After mounting a cloud with his legionnaires, Monkey called up a gale to blow them swiftly back to their home, where he distributed the weapons to his army of little ones.

The next day all the monkeys gathered in formation as usual, but now they had real weapons to train with, and it wasn't long before their mountain fortress had become as strong as a good iron bucket or a city of metal. With an arsenal to choose from, each of the monkeys soon became proficient with his chosen weapon. But Monkey's sword did not please him. Calling on his trusted aides, he said, "This weapon is too cumbersome, it does not suit me. What am I to do?"

"It is understandable," they said, "that you would be dissatisfied with such an earthly weapon. His Majesty is a divine sage and therefore requires a weapon befitting an immortal. We suggest that you visit the denizens of the sea. Providing, of course, that Your Majesty is able to travel through water."

Monkey said, "Since my illumination I have been able to embody seventy-two transformations, which includes the unlimited power of the cloud somersault, the magic of body displacement, and concealment, which allows me to hide myself in other forms or to vanish entirely. I can travel to Heaven or enter the Earth. I can zoom past the sun and the moon without casting a shadow. I can penetrate stone and metal; fire cannot burn me nor water drown me. There is no place, known or unknown, that I cannot enter or go to."

"In that case, there should be no problem. To reach the Dragon Palace of the Eastern Ocean, you have merely to follow the waters flowing under our iron bridge. No doubt the Dragon King will be able to provide a suitable weapon for his Majesty."

Monkey mounted the bridgehead, clenched his fists in a special manner to protect himself against the water powers, invoked the magic spell, and dove into the current. Following the waterway, he soon reached the Eastern Ocean, where he was stopped by a demon who was patrolling the waters. "What kind of sage or divinity are you, that you can walk through water as casually as if you were on land? Account for yourself and give me your name, that I may report you to the powers that be."

"I am the Handsome Monkey King of the Mountain of Flowers and Fruit, a near neighbor of the Dragon King. I have come to make his acquaintance."

The demon turned on his heels and sped to the Water Crystal Palace to make his report.

Ao-kuang, the Dragon King of the Eastern Ocean, came to the door of the palace to welcome the Monkey King. He was followed by his shrimp soldiers and crab generals. "Come in, exalted Immortal," he said, addressing Monkey. Ao-kuang led the way to the dais, where they were able to converse in private. After tea had been served, the Dragon King asked Monkey, "How long have you been on the Way, and what are the magic arts you have acquired?"

"I have been on the Way for nearly all of my life," Monkey replied, "and I am now an immortal, having broken the chains of samsara. In recent days I have been training my subjects in the arts of self-defense, but I have not yet found an appropriate weapon for myself. I have been advised that you, my illustrious neighbor residing within the shell portals of the Green Jade Palace, would be able to provide me with a weapon suitable to my station and my needs."

The Dragon King was beginning to feel uneasy, but he did not see how he could turn down Monkey's request. He called forth his perch commander and ordered him to bring a large sword. "That's not the weapon for me," Monkey said, taking it in his hand and making an imaginary parry. "Don't like it, don't like it, bring me something else."

The Dragon King sent a whiting lieutenant and an eel porter to bring a nine-pronged fork. This time Monkey leapt down from the dais and made several jabs and thrusts with the fork. "Much too light," Monkey said, "and it doesn't suit my hand. Find me something else."

The Dragon King cleared his throat. "Have a closer look, Monkey King. That fork weighs 3,600 pounds."

"Doesn't suit my hand, doesn't suit my hand."

The Dragon King was becoming worried. He ordered a bream admiral and a carp brigadier to bring forth a giant halberd, weighing 7,200 pounds. Monkey jumped forward and took hold of it. After a few thrusts and parries he put it down. "Still too light! Much too light!"

"But that's our heaviest weapon!" the Dragon King exclaimed.

Monkey replied, "As the saying goes, 'There is no need to worry about the Dragon King lacking treasures.' Have another look around, and if you can find me the right weapon I will make it worth your while."

"There are no more weapons to be found in the Palace," the Dragon King replied. While they were speaking, the Dragon Mother and her daughters had entered the room from the back of the palace. Taking her husband aside, she whispered, "This is no ordinary sage to be appeased with commonplace armaments. In our treasury is a rare piece of magic iron that once anchored the Milky Way. Of late it has taken on a rosy glow and casts an auspicious light. Can this be a sign that it is to be taken by our visitor, the divine sage?"

"That iron," the Dragon King said, "was the instrument used by the Great Yu when he pounded the depths of the great rivers and oceans into place and subdued the Flood. Of what use could a holy piece of iron be to the Monkey King?"

"Let's not worry about that," the Dragon Mother answered. "If he likes it, let him take it away and leave us in peace."

The Dragon King finally agreed and told Monkey of the history of the iron, hoping to impress him. "Go get it," Monkey said, "and let me have a look!"

"We can't do that," the Dragon King said, "it's too heavy. Come with us and we will show it to you."

Monkey was led to the Ocean Treasury. Even as they approached from a distance they were made aware of its shining presence. "There it is," the Dragon King boasted, "casting forth a thousand rays of golden light." Monkey braced himself and approached the rare object. It was an iron rod, thick as a pillar, and about seventy feet in length. Monkey seized it with both hands. "Too thick and long," he said, but the words were hardly out of his mouth when the rod became two feet shorter and a little thinner. "That's better," Monkey said, "but a little shorter and also a little thinner would be even better." Once again the rod shrank. Monkey gave it a bounce and walked out of the treasury for a closer examination. "Still not right, not quite right," he said under his breath. The rod instantly became twenty feet in length, with a perfectly corresponding width.

As Monkey walked back to the Water Crystal Palace he made several thrusts and passes, engaging in mock combat. The Dragon King shook with fear at the sight of Monkey, and all the Dragon Princesses covered their faces and tried to hide. Terrapins and sea turtles drew in their heads, while the shrimps, crabs, and fishes all went into hiding.

Once again Monkey sat down beside the Dragon King, after first reducing his cudgel to the size of a needle and placing it behind his ear. "I'm deeply grateful to my good neighbor for his immeasurable kindness," he said.

"Don't mention it," the Dragon King said. "Glad to be of service."

"I have one more request to make," Monkey said.

"What might that be?"

"Well," Monkey began, "before I had this magic cudgel it was one thing, now that I have it, it is another."

"How is that, exalted immortal?"

"All at once I find myself improperly dressed. What does the Dragon Palace hold in the way of martial apparel?"

"Why, nothing at all," the Dragon King replied. "We've never gone in for combat attire."

"You know the old saying, 'One guest should not trouble two hosts.' "

"Just as you say," the Dragon King replied, "but in this instance it might be better to try another ocean treasury."

"I have no intention of leaving before I get what I want."

"If I had what you wanted, I would have presented it to you by now," the Dragon King said, growing noticeably nervous.

"Is that so?" Monkey shouted. "Perhaps I should try this iron cudgel on you!"

"Hold it! Hold it!" the Dragon King gasped. "I'm sure one of my brothers will be able to fix you up."

"Who are your honored brothers, and where do they live?"

"They are Ao-ch'in, Dragon King of the Southern Ocean, Ao-shun, Dragon King of the Northern Ocean, and Ao-jun, Dragon King of the Western Ocean."

"It's out of the question my going to them. You know the proverb, 'Two mussels on the rock are better than three underneath.' "

"I wasn't suggesting you go anywhere. In the palace I have an iron drum and a bronze bell. In an emergency I have only to beat the drum and strike the bell and my brothers come running."

"In that case, have it done, have it done."

A crocodile was called to beat the drum, and a tortoise, to sound the bell. In an instant, as the Dragon King had promised, the three brothers appeared in the outer courtyard, where they were met by the Dragon King of the Water Crystal Palace. "Elder Brother," said Ao-ch'in, "why have you called us here? I can see by the look on your face that all is not well."

"Brother, I am glad you have asked. A troublesome neighbor of mine, who rules over the Mountain of Flowers and Fruit, has come here in search of a magic weapon for his personal use. Unable to please him, I finally turned over the iron that fixed the Milky Way into place, which he instantly transformed into a death-dealing cudgel. Now he wants an appropriate garment to go with his weapon, some sort of battle dress. I have nothing like that here. If one of you can get him outfitted to his liking, we can get rid of him."

While the brothers talked, they could see Monkey inside the palace, strutting his stuff and slaying imaginary armies with his iron cudgel.

Ao-ch'in became furious when he realized that the intruder was only a monkey. "Let's call our armies together and take him captive."

"Not so fast, honored brother," Ao-kuang said. "I failed to tell you that the Monkey King is an immortal, and that iron cudgel in his hand is a deadly weapon."

Ao-jun then spoke. "Second Elder Brother spoke too quickly. Let's put a suitable outfit together and get that ape off our property. Once we are rid of him we'll send a formal complaint to Heaven and let them take care of it in their own manner."

"Good idea," Ao-shun said. "I have here a pair of cloud-treading shoes made of root fiber."

Said Ao-jun, "I have with me a cuirass of chain mail made of yellow gold."

"I have a phoenix plume hat made of red gold," said Ao-ch'in.

The Dragon King was delighted. He gathered the garments and entered the Water Crystal Palace, where he presented them to Monkey.

Monkey donned his new outfit and, feigning combat, tripped out of the palace. He headed for home without so much as a word of thanks to the Dragon Kings at the gate, who shook their heads in disgust.

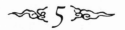

A Messenger from Heaven

*T*HE Jade Emperor was sitting on his throne in the Treasure
Hall of Divine Mists in the Cloud Palace of Golden Arches,
surrounded by his immortal ministers, civil and military. It
was the hour of the morning report. One of the members
announced, "Your Holiness, Ao-kuang, Dragon of the Eastern
Ocean, has presented a memorial outside the Hall of Universal
Brightness and awaits your command."

Ao-kuang was ushered into the great hall, where he presented his summons to the Jade Emperor. "Tell us in your
own words what is in the summons," the Emperor commanded, "that we may all hear it together."

"Your Highest and Holiest," Ao-kuang began, "your
humble servant wishes to inform the Wise Lord of Heaven
that a certain monkey king from the Mountain of Flowers and
Fruit—a most suspicious-acting immortal—forced his way
into our treasury and through the use of violence and intim-
idation demanded a weapon and garments. He terrorized my
watery kinsman, causing the tortoises and alligators to flee in
terror. The Dragon of the Southern Ocean trembled, the
Dragon of the Western Ocean was horror-struck, the Dragon
of the Northern Ocean was humiliated, and your subject Ao-
kuang was brought to his knees by Monkey's might. We of
the Eastern Ocean presented him with a magic iron, which he
transformed into a death-dealing cudgel, and my brothers outfitted him in cloud-stepping shoes, a coat of chain mail, and a

*The Dragon King in the Treasure Hall of Divine Mists
in the Cloud Palace of Golden Arches*

phoenix plume cap. We sent him off with great courtesy, but all he did was swagger and boast. He offered us not even a word of thanks. We are no match for him, and so we earnestly beseech our Lord to deal with this menace, that the Lower Regions may once again live in peace and prosperity."

When Ao-kuang had concluded his plea, the Jade Emperor said, "The Dragon King is to return to the sea, and I will send one of our generals to arrest this monkey fiend."

After the Dragon King had made his obeisance and left, the Jade Emperor asked his ministers, "When was this pernicious little monkey born, and how did he come to be an immortal?" Thousand-League Eye and Down-the-Wind Ears stepped forward. "This is the stone monkey born of Heaven. There was nothing extraordinary about him at first, but of late he has acquired the properties of an immortal, no one knows how. Now he subdues dragons and tames tigers."

"Which of our divine generals should we send down to corral this troublesome ape?"

Gold Star, the spirit of the Planet Venus stepped forward. "Highest and Holiest," he said, "all creatures endowed with the nine apertures are endowed with the possibility of achieving immortality. We should not be surprised then that this monkey with a body produced by the natural forces of Heaven and Earth and conceived by the Sun and the Moon should achieve immortality, for does his head not point to the Heavens, and with his feet does he not trod upon the Earth, and does he not feed on dew and mist? Further, Your Holiness, his ability to subdue dragons and tame tigers makes him the equal of humans. I think, therefore, that we should take a compassionate course by summoning him to the Upper Regions and record his name in the Register. That way we can control him, and by giving him official work we can keep an eye on him. If he obeys Your Heavenly command he will be promoted, and if not he will be arrested. Such diplomacy will spare us a military expedition and will also provide us with an immortal."

The Jade Emperor was pleased. He ordered one of the Star Spirits of Song to compose the edict, and the spirit of Planet Venus to deliver it. Leaving by the southern gate, the Planet Venus lowered his hallowed cloud and soon reached the Water Curtain Cave. He told the monkeys who crowded around him there that he was a messenger from Heaven, and that he had come to summon their king to the Upper Regions. The little monkeys quickly relayed the message. Upon hearing the summons, Monkey said, "How very timely! It has been on my mind in recent days that perhaps the time had come for me to make a trip to Heaven."

The Handsome Monkey King was led by the Planet Venus into the Treasure Hall of Divine Mists. They went before the Imperial Presence without being announced. Gold Star performed obeisance to the throne, but Monkey merely stood at his side without showing respect, only pricking his ears so as not to miss anything.

"In accordance with the Divine Edict, I am here to deliver to His Presence this troublesome demon."

Having lowered his curtain, the Jade Emperor asked, "Which one is the demon?"

Monkey bowed slightly. "It is I."

The divine ministers blanched with horror. "Who is this savage ape who not only does not prostrate himself before the Presence but who speaks without permission and has the audacity to say, 'It is I'? There is only one fitting punishment for such audacity: death!"

The Jade Emperor listened patiently to his ministers.

"This demon is an immortal from the Lower Regions who has only recently taken a humanlike form. For now we must pardon him, for he does not understand court procedures."

The divine ministers bowed before the Presence and commended the Jade Emperor for his clemency, who then ordered them to find an appointment for Monkey. "All of the departments are full," they said.

"In that case," the Jade Emperor said, "we will make him *pi-ma-wen* in the stables."

Monkey wasted no time in taking command of the stables. Gathering his staff together, he made a tour of the grounds. One thousand horses were in his charge, all of them under the care of a steward who saw to their fodder. There were several grooms to chop hay, fetch water, and comb and bathe the horses. The accountants were in charge of supplies. In addition, a superintendent and his assistant were to help Monkey in seeing to the general management of the stables.

The heavenly horses responded favorably to Monkey's presence. Whenever they saw him they would prick up their ears and paw the ground. Their appetites increased, and they soon became fat and saucy.

A fortnight passed in this fashion. One day the officers announced that there would be a party to officially welcome Monkey to his post. It was a splendid occasion, and Monkey, as might be expected, was very happy with himself. Seated at the banquet table, raising his cup to his lips, he suddenly paused and said, "What is the meaning of my title? What does the word *pi-ma-wen* mean, and what is my rank?"

"The rank and title are identical," the officers said.

"But what classification is it?"

"It doesn't come under any classification."

"It's too high to be counted as a class, is that it?" Monkey said.

"Quite the opposite, it is that it is too low."

"Too low!" Monkey exclaimed. "How can that be?"

"Well," they replied, "it is like this: when a minister is too low to be classed, then he is given the job of tending horses. We have seen this happen before. For example, you have done an excellent job thus far, and for this you will get a mark of 'not so bad.' But if the horses were to grow wan, if they were to become disspirited, why, you would be rebuked. And if any harm were to come to them, then you would be persecuted and fined."

Fire leapt out of Monkey's eyes and nostrils. He gnashed his teeth and growled, "So that's what they think of Monkey! Aren't they aware that on the Mountain of Flowers and Fruit I am King and Patriarch? How dare they trick me into taking this lowly job? No sir, not me! Not this monkey!" And with that he overturned the table at which he was sitting and bounded from the premises.

Monkey next rushed to the Southern Gate and, ignoring the deities on guard, made the magic pass and somersaulted into space. When he reached the Mountain of Flowers and Fruit, he lowered his cloud and shouted, "Little ones, your Handsome Monkey King has returned." After they had kowtowed and led Monkey to his sacred quarters in the cave, his subjects began preparations for a banquet to honor and celebrate their leader.

As the banquet was about to begin, they turned to Monkey and said, "Since you have been gone ten years, it is assumed you have had great success."

"What do you mean, ten years?" Monkey said. "It is barely two weeks!"

"Apparently you didn't notice. It is said that a day in Heaven is like a year below. Please tell us, what was your office and rank in the Upper Regions?"

"Don't bring it up," Monkey said. "The humiliation is too great. I was given a menial job with no rank. But once I caught on I got out fast."

"Just as well!" the monkeys applauded, "just as well! Why be ruled up there when you can be the ruler down here?"

"Little ones," Monkey said, "bring the wine quickly, and cheer up your King."

In the Cloud Palace of the Jade Emperor

*I*N the following day Monkey issued an official proclama-
tion that henceforth he would be referred to as "Great
Sage, Equal of Heaven." He ordered his generals to set up a
banner to herald his new title.

At the same moment that Monkey was being trumpeted
on his mountain, the Jade Emperor was holding his morning
court. During the session the superintendent of the Heavenly
Stables intervened to announce that Monkey had left in a huff
on the previous day upon learning the true meaning and value
of his title, *pi-ma-wen.* "Further," the superintendent explained, "we have learned that he left by way of the Heavenly
Gate, presumably to return to his home."

The Jade Emperor dismissed the superintendent, saying,
"I shall send my celestial soldiers to capture that monster."
Devaraja Li, the Pagoda-Bearing Heavenly King, and his son,
Natha, stepped forward at once and volunteered their services.
They were immediately placed in charge of the campaign, and
after reviewing the troops they appointed the god Mighty-
Mighty to lead the vanguard and the Fish-Belly General to
bring up the rear, while the General of the Yakshas was to lead
the troops on.

They left by the Southern Gate and were soon in sight of
the Mountain of Flowers and Fruit. After finding level ground
for their encampment, General Mighty-Mighty was elected to
issue the challenge of battle. He quickly buckled up his armor

and, clutching his great battle ax, sallied forth in the direction of the Water Curtain Cave.

At the cave entrance he was confronted by a band of monsters—wolves, tigers, leopards, and the like—prancing and jumping, growling and brandishing spears and swords, and brawling with one another in mock combat. "You troublesome beasts," cried Mighty-Mighty, "go forward at once and tell that horse-grooming king of yours that a Heavenly general has come to subdue him on orders from the Jade Emperor. If he doesn't surrender at once you will all be annihilated!"

The monsters rushed into the cave and prostrated themselves before Monkey. "Disaster! Disaster!" they shouted.

"Steady, steady," Monkey roared back. "What sort of disaster?"

"There's a Heavenly general outside who has come on orders from the Jade Emperor. If you don't surrender at once we will all be destroyed."

"What rot!" Monkey said. "Bring me my battle dress at once!" Monkey slipped into his cloud-stepping shoes, his bronze helmet, and his golden corselet, and with his magic cudgel in hand he led his troops outside and arranged them in battle formation.

Mighty-Mighty shouted, "You lawless ape, don't look aside as if you don't see me and don't know who I am."

"Which little deity are *you?*" Monkey asked. "You'd best tell me your name if you want to be recognized."

"You insolent ape, I am the vanguard commander, the Celestial General Mighty-Mighty."

"What's all that title-slinging to me?" Monkey said. "I am the Great Sage, Equal of Heaven."

"Don't make me laugh! If you and your pygmy monsters want to live, you had better surrender at once and throw yourselves at the mercy of the Heavenly Court. If you so much as breathe half a 'no,' I will cut you to ribbons and trample your bones to dust."

"You can't threaten me, you puny little deity. I would kill you at once if I didn't need you to carry a message to the Jade Emperor. Go tell him that he doesn't respect real talent. Doesn't he understand that I am in possession of real magic? How could he ask me to be a mere groomer of horses? See what is written on this banner! If he will accede to this title and make it official, I will leave him in peace, but if not I will return to the Treasure Hall of Divine Mists and make such a row as will knock him off his couch."

Mighty-Mighty looked incredulously from Monkey to the banner and burst out laughing. "*You* the equal of Heaven!" he stormed. "Why, you impudent fiend! Open your mouth this one last time and have a taste of my ax!" Monkey raised his cudgel in plenty of time to deflect the blow, and they went at each other, trading blow for blow without anyone showing the least advantage. It wasn't long before Mighty-Mighty began to weaken. Defending a mighty blow to his head from Monkey's cudgel, his ax split in two, and he had to run for his life.

When Mighty-Mighty returned to camp and confessed to the humiliating defeat he had suffered at Monkey's hands, Devaraja Li was outraged and ordered that Mighty-Mighty be taken away and executed. But his son Natha stepped forward and said, "Spare Mighty-Mighty, father, until I have engaged the horse groomer on my own terms." Devaraja Li consented, and Mighty-Mighty was returned to camp to await trial while Natha prepared for battle.

Monkey was dismissing his troops when he turned to see Prince Natha approaching, casting spells and performing transformations in the air as he came, with three divine weapons in each hand. When the young Prince landed at Monkey's feet, Monkey said, "Whose little boy is this?"

"You don't know who I am, you nauseating monkey fiend. I am Natha, third son of the Pagoda-Bearing Heavenly King. I have come here under orders of the Jade Emperor to take you into custody."

"Little prince," Monkey said, a grin spreading over his face, "your baby teeth are still in place, and your natal hair is still damp. Don't make me laugh! I will spare your life, but you must report the words on this banner to the Jade Emperor, and if he will concede that rank, your army can return in peace and I will submit on my own. But if not, I'll come up there and blast the Jewel Palace."

Prince Natha looked up at the banner and read the words *Great Sage, Equal of Heaven*. "You stinking little monkey, what powers do you possess that you could lay claim to such a title? We'll settle this with one blow of my sword."

"Be my guest," Monkey said, and stood his ground. "If you have swords to spare, then I have swords to break."

Furious, Natha cried, "Change!" whereupon he was transformed into a ferocious deity with three heads and six arms. His hands held six weapons: a monster-slashing sword, a monster-hacking scimitar, a monster-binding rope, a monster-quelling club, an embroidered ball, and a fire wheel. Brandishing these weapons, he charged Monkey.

"So you've a trick or two up your sleeve," Monkey said. "Well, have a look at this!" Shouting "Change!" Monkey turned into a demon with three heads and six arms. His cudgel had become three cudgels, and grabbing each with two hands, he engaged Natha in an earth-shaking, mountain-trembling battle. They flew through the air like meteors and clashed like lightning, each parry and blow a thunderclap, with sparks flashing across the skies like shooting stars.

The battle had gone thirty rounds without anyone gaining the advantage. The six weapons of Natha changed from one thousand to ten thousand pieces and then back again, with Monkey's cudgel doing the same. But in the end Monkey proved to be the warrior with the swifter eye and hand. While creating a double of himself to battle Natha, he slipped behind the prince, who was in the midst of another transformation himself. Before Natha could catch himself he heard the whir of Monkey's cudgel behind his left ear, followed by a crashing blow to his shoulder. Terrorized and in pain, he changed back into his natural form, gathered his weapons, and fled back to his camp.

Vaishravana had been watching the battle from a distance. His son now stood before him, trembling and drained of color. "My father and king," the prince said, "the horse groomer has great powers. My magic was no match for his."

"If he has powers like that, how will we ever defeat him?"

"On a pole outside his cave is a banner that bears the words *Great Sage, Equal of Heaven*. This is how that audacious monkey views himself. He says that if we will acknowledge his title in Heaven he will return with us of his own accord. But if not, he plans to terrorize the Treasure Hall of Divine Mists."

"In that case, we had better return and make our report to the Jade Emperor, who will surely send reinforcements and conquer the fiend."

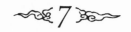

Immortality Peaches and Golden Elixirs

*A*T the same moment that Monkey and his little ones were banqueting and celebrating their great victory over the deities of Heaven, the Jade Emperor was admonishing his troops for failing to bring Monkey to bay. "How dare this baneful monkey be so insolent as to believe himself to be, as he says, 'Great Sage, Equal of Heaven'? I will order my top generals to execute him at once."

The spirit of the Planet Venus stepped forward. "Your Majesty," the Gold Star said, "this unseemly monkey knows how to brag, but he is lacking in propriety and good sense alike. Yet if we were to engage him in battle it would greatly tax our strength. Perhaps a more cautionary move would be to grant him the title that he insists upon, which is after all a rank without compensation."

"What do you mean, a rank without compensation?"

"I mean that the title is not official but empty, in that no duties are attached to it; furthermore, he will not be paid. We shall keep him in Heaven, where we can keep an eye on him, and in this way both Heaven and Earth will be at peace."

The Jade Emperor looked around the room at the strained and anxious faces of his aides, while he considered what should be done. At last he said, "We will follow the wise counsel of Gold Star."

The Heavenly Factotums Chang and Lu were appointed to build the official quarters of the Great Sage, Equal of Heaven, just to the right of the Garden of Immortal Peaches. Within Monkey's offices there were to be two departments, one called Peace and Quiet, and the other, Serene Spirit, and each would have attending officials. Monkey was accompanied to his post by several star spirits, who presented him with ten stems of golden flowers. He was also given his first ration of two bottles of Imperial wine, which would henceforth be his daily allowance. After they had admonished Monkey to control himself and refrain from outrageous behavior, the star spirits excused themselves and returned to their posts, whereupon Monkey immediately uncorked the two bottles of wine and invited his officers to a feast.

From that day forth Monkey gave no more thought to title, rank, or salary. He was satisfied—at least for the time being—that his name had been placed on the register. Since all his needs were answered for, he had little to think about besides his meals, and nothing to contemplate but his freedom and leisure. He therefore took to wandering about Heaven, where he made friends of the various denizens. He was careful to address each member of the Trinity as "Your Reverence," and each of the Four Emperors as "Your Majesty," but the others—the stars, constellations, and planets and the countless gods of the Milky Way— he addressed as equals.

One day at court, one of the Jade Emperor's ministers said, "The Great Sage, Equal of Heaven, is in his idleness beginning to wander through the Heavens, making friends with all he meets and treating them as cronies regardless of their rank. If we don't curtail his wanderings and give him an assignment it will just be a matter of time before he will again make mischief."

The Jade Emperor sent for Monkey at once. "What's the

good news?" Monkey intoned, upon reporting to His Presence. "Another promotion or reward, or did you want to elevate my rank?"

The Jade Emperor concealed his irritation. "It has come to my attention," he said, "that you have been leading a life of irresponsible indolence. I have decided therefore to give you a temporary assignment. You are to look after the Garden of Immortal Peaches. I will expect you to give this your full attention. It is an important position, not to be taken lightly."

Monkey was delighted. Grunting his thanks, he bowed deeply, withdrew, and flew off to the garden. There he was stopped by a local spirit who, motioning Monkey to halt, asked him where he was hurrying off to.

"The Jade Emperor has just put me in charge of the peaches," Monkey replied. "I'm going to inspect my garden."

After saluting properly, the local spirit called to all the stewards in charge of watering, hoeing, sweeping, and tending the peach trees to come forward and kowtow to the Great Sage. Then they led him ceremoniously into the Immortal Peach Garden.

Monkey took in the green and orderly scene that stretched out before him. "How many peach trees are there?" he asked the spirit.

"There are 3,600," the spirit said. "In the front garden are 1,200 trees with tiny flowers that bear small fruit. These ripen every three thousand years. To eat but one peach is to become immortal, with full knowledge of the Way. In the center garden are 1,200 trees, each of these having multiple blossoms and succulent fruits that ripen every six thousand years. Whoever eats of these will ascend to Heaven on a cloud and enjoy eternal youth. At the back of the garden are 1,200 trees whose fruit is purple-veined, with pale yellow pits. These ripen once in nine thousand years. If eaten, they will make one as eternal as Heaven and Earth, and the equal of Sun and Moon."

Monkey was truly pleased. After dismissing the spirit, he made a thorough inspection of the trees and made a listing of the arbors and pagodas before returning to his residence. From that day on he went to the orchards every three or four days to enjoy the scenery and to casually inspect the grounds. He stopped seeing his many friends and no longer took any journeys.

One day he saw that a group of trees in the back garden bore fruit that was beginning to ripen. Monkey was very curious to sample the taste of these immortal peaches. Unfortunately, his stewards and the local spirit were always lurking about. To shake them off, he said, "Why don't you take leave of me and wait outside the garden, while I rest in this arbor?" After they had withdrawn, Monkey took off his official robe and cap and climbed into the branches of the tallest tree. After plucking several of the ripest peaches he could find, he sat astride an upper branch and munched on them to his heart's content.

This naughty habit, once begun, was repeated every three or four days. One morning, her Majesty the Queen Mother decided to give a Peach Banquet to celebrate the Grand Festival of Immortal Peaches. The fairy maidens in their various-colored jackets were to fill their baskets with peaches from the Immortal Peach Garden. When the seven maidens arrived at the gate of the garden they found it guarded by the local spirit and his attendants. The local spirit stopped them at the gate. "Things have changed this year," he said. "The Great Sage, Equal of Heaven, is now in charge of the garden. We shall need his permission before we can allow you to enter."

"Where is the Great Sage?" asked the maidens.

"He is in the garden," the local spirit replied. "He has grown tired and is taking a nap in one of the arbors."

"Please go and find him at once. We must not be late for the Queen Mother." But when they went to search for Monkey they could find nothing but his hat and robe. Monkey, of course, had climbed one of the trees and, after eating his fill and reducing himself in size to a mere two inches, was now fast asleep in a curled-up leaf.

The fairy maidens came marching into the garden behind the attendants and announced, "We are here by Imperial Decree and cannot go back empty-handed."

The local spirit nodded. "The Great Sage has no doubt wandered off somewhere, but he is bound to turn up soon. I see no reason to delay Her Majesty's celebration. We will make a full report to the Great Sage upon his return."

The fairy maidens picked two basketfuls from the trees in front, and three more from the trees in the middle, but when they reached the back of the garden all the peaches were green. Several of the trees had broken branches. They were about to leave the garden when one of the maidens spotted a ripe peach on a lower branch. The Blue-Gown Maiden pulled the branch down while the Red-Gown Maiden plucked the fruit. This was the very branch on which Monkey had been snoozing! When the Blue-Gown Maiden let go of the branch and it snapped back into place, Monkey went flying into space. But in an instant he recovered, changed back into his actual size, and came floating back to earth. "Thieves! Robbers!" he cried out. "What are you doing in my garden, you peach-eating monsters?"

The maidens cowered before Monkey and fell to their knees. "Please, Great Sage," they pleaded, "we are no monsters but rather the Seven-Gown Immortal Maidens sent by the Queen Mother to gather peaches for the annual festival."

Monkey's anger turned to instant delight. "Well, get off your knees then and tell the Great Sage about the Queen Mother's party. Who's been invited?"

"That's an official matter," they said. "It's all according to rule, you know. The Buddha will be there, of course, along with the Bodhisattvas, the Holy Monks, the Arhats, Kuan-yin from the South Pole, the Venerable Immortals of the Ten Continents and its Three Islands, the Mystic Divinity of the North Pole, and the Great Immortal of the Yellow Horn. There will also be the Star Lords of the Five Constellations, the Three Pure Ones, the Four Emperors and the Heavenly Immortal of the Great Nomad from the Eight High Caves, the Jade Emperor, naturally, and the Immortal of the Nine Mounds, the Gods of the Seas and Mountains, and the Ruler of the Nether World from the Eight Lower Caves. Also the terrestrial deities. These and the major and minor gods of the halls and palaces will all be invited to the feast."

"How about me?" Monkey smiled. "Of course I too will be invited?"

"Your name has never been mentioned."

"What do you mean?" Monkey roared. "I am the Great Sage, Equal of Heaven! How can they leave me out? I should be an honored guest."

"We were simply telling you who was invited according to the old rule. We don't know who will be invited this time."

"Quite right, my dears. I'm not blaming you. The Great Sage will look into this on his own." Monkey made a magic sign, recited a spell, and said to the maidens, "Stay! Stay! Stay!" The maidens, their eyes wide open, were transfixed to the spot. Monkey leaped onto his magic cloud and headed straight for the Green Jade Pool. Because he wasn't paying attention, his cloud nearly collided with the cloud of the Barefoot Immortal. "How propitious," Monkey thought, and conceived a plan on the spot to fool the old immortal. "Where are you headed, Venerable Wisdom?" Monkey enquired.

"Why, to the Peach Banquet."

"You must not have heard," Monkey said. "Thanks to my swift cloud-somersaulting, the Jade Emperor has asked me to convey a message to all the honored guests. Before going to the Green Jade Pool, all the immortals are to go to the Hall of Bright Lights for a rehearsal of ceremonies before proceeding to the banquet."

For all his wisdom, the Barefoot Immortal was a naive man. "That's not how we did it in the past," he said. But when Monkey stared back at him without uttering another word, the old immortal turned his cloud to the left and was soon out of sight.

Monkey headed straight for the Green Jade Pool. Reciting a spell, he shook himself and turned into a perfect replica of the Barefoot Immortal. He stopped his cloud at the Chamber of Treasures and walked quietly inside. Monkey was the first to arrive. Leaning against the door, he gazed in amazement at the festive decorations. Waves of perfume wafted throughout the halls, comingling with layers of holy mist. The jade terrace was arrayed with ornaments, each one representing an aspect of the life force. A phoenix, ethereal in form, appeared to rise up through the glass-domed roof. Golden blossoms on stems of green jade surrounded a nine-phoenix screen. Green jade bowls with a thousand flowers adorned an inlaid gold table, holding delicacies in abundance: dragon livers and phoenix marrow, bear paws and ape lips, rabbit embryo, carp tail, broiled osprey, and kumiss, all decorated with various fruits.

While Monkey continued to peer in from the door, slowly, almost imperceptibly, the odor of newly fermented wine reached his nostrils. The ministrants were making wine in the halls, some carrying mashed grains, others bringing in water, while jugs were being washed and barrels scrubbed clean. Monkey began to salivate. Longing to taste the wine, he forgot himself. Without another thought, he plucked several hairs from his body, threw them in his mouth, and spit out the chewed pieces, chanting, "Change! Change!" All at once the room was filled with sleep-inducing insects that alighted on the faces of the workers. In an instant everyone in the hall was fast asleep but Monkey, who ran to the golden table and gathered an armful of delicacies. Then he raced into the gallery. Sitting beside the filled wine bottles and leaning against the jugs, he stuffed his face with food and tilted a jug to his lips. Now sated and thoroughly drunk, Monkey staggered to his feet and looked around. "Oh, this is bad, very bad! Soon the guests will be here and I will be found out. I had better get back to my quarters and sleep it off."

Monkey staggered out the door and stumbled along the pathway, soon losing his way. Instead of returning to his official residence, he found himself by mistake in the Tushita Palace. "How did I get here?" Monkey asked himself. "This is the home of Lao-tzu. Well, never mind. I always wanted to meet the old man, and here's my opportunity." Standing before the entrance, he brushed off his clothes, collected himself, and pushed open the door. But Lao-tzu was nowhere to be seen. Monkey lurched through the rooms until he came to a passageway that led to Lao-tzu's alchemical laboratory. He was immediately attracted to an oven fire beside the hearth. Five gourds were placed around the fire, each filled with finished elixir. "This is the supreme treasure of the immortals," Monkey said. "Fancy, I was about to produce a little golden elixir on my own, had I not been so busy with other matters. But here's opportunity knocking at my door." With no more thought than that, Monkey tilted the gourds one by one and drank up the refined pills they contained as if they had been no more than a dish of fried beans.

The unearthly and very potent results of the pills soon dispelled the effects of the wine. "Oh bad, bad," Monkey said, "this little escapade is even worse than the last one. If Lao-tzu catches me it could mean the end of my life. Better a king of monkeys in the world below than a dead ape up here!" Casting a spell that rendered him invisible, Monkey quickly somersaulted onto his getaway cloud and left by the Western Gate.

When Monkey's cloud descended to his home in the Mountain of Flowers and Fruit, he was greeted by streaming banners and glinting spears. "Little ones," Monkey called out, "your King has come home." The monkeys threw down their spears and halberds, flags and banners, and, forgetting their war games, fell on their knees before the Handsome Monkey King. After scolding Monkey for leaving them, they immediately set about preparing a banquet in his honor.

As the banquet was about to get under way, Monkey was given a bowl of coconut wine to toast the ceremonial gathering. He took one sip, put the bowl down, and made a face. "What is the matter, Your Majesty?" they asked.

"I can't drink this stuff. It's awful, just awful!"

Peng and Pa, his two stalwart generals, came forward and said, "Now that Your Majesty has become accustomed to immortal libations and Heavenly morsels of food, it is no wonder you find mortal fare distasteful. But perhaps we should remember the proverb that says, 'Sweet or sour, it's water from home.'"

"It's true," Monkey said, "and there are no people like home people. Still, this morning at the Green Jade Pool in Heaven, I savored wine of the Heavens. There is no help for it; I shall have to return and steal a few bottles, so that you can taste the wine to which I have become accustomed. Just half a cup each and none of you will grow old."

When Monkey returned to the Chamber of Treasures, he found the ministrants still sound asleep, with the banquet yet to get under way. Monkey put one large bottle under each arm and grabbed two more with his hands. Leaping back onto his cloud, he returned to his home.

Monkey Goes Too Far

*T*HE Jade Emperor, sitting at Court, began receiving a wave of disturbing reports: the seven maidens, released at last from their spell, were milling about in the corridor, waiting to make their report. They were followed by the ministers, who reported the stolen wine. No sooner had these parties departed when one of Monkey's attendants reported that the Great Sage was missing. Just then the arrival of Lao-tzu was announced. He was ushered in before the Jade Emperor, who was eager for him to speak. "I am sorry to report that the Golden Elixir I had been preparing for the Grand Festival of Cinnibar has been stolen." The Jade Emperor was more than a little suspicious as to the identity of the culprit. Just then the Barefoot Immortal was ushered in. "I was on the way to the Peach Banquet, Your Majesty, when I bumped into the Great Sage, Equal of Heaven. He informed me that all the guests were to rehearse the ceremonies of the banquet at the Hall of Penetrating Light. I was waiting there—"

"Enough! Enough!" roared the Jade Emperor, interrupting the Barefoot Immortal. Turning to one of his ministers, he said, "Get the Celestial Investigator on the track of that incorrigible baboon. I want a full investigation conducted at once!"

To no one's surprise, the investigative report revealed the true identity of the culprit who was responsible for each of the reported misdeeds. The Jade Emperor decided to rid himself of Monkey once and for all. He commanded the Kings of the

Four Quarters to assist Vaishravana and Prince Natha. They would be followed in a chain of command by the Twenty-eight Constellations, the Nine Planets, the Twelve Hoary Branches, the Fearless Guards of the Five Quarters, the Four Temporal Guardians, the Stars of East and West, the Gods of North and South, the Deities of the Five Mountains and the Four Rivers, the Star Spirits of the entire Heaven, and a hundred thousand celestial soldiers. When they reached the Mountain of Flowers and Fruit, they were to set up an eighteen-branched cosmic net to encircle Monkey's domain and insure his capture.

Once everything was in place, the Nine Planets stepped forward to present the challenge. Monkey was inside with his generals, finishing off the last of the Heavenly wine. When the little ones rushed in with the news of another impending disaster, Monkey refused to stir from his throne. "No disturbance can equal in importance the pleasure of wine; nor should any worry quell the afterglow of the sacred grape." But hardly were these words out of his mouth before another squad of imps entered to plead, "Your Majesty, they are threatening war and destruction, we are surrounded and outnumbered!"

"Poetry and wine can confer such glory upon an hour that fame and fortune must wait its day," Monkey intoned. But yet a further wave of imps rushed in. "Holy King," they implored, "those savage deities have broken down the door and are fighting their way inside."

"I have no quarrel with those goons," Monkey said, "but because of their bad manners I have no choice." He gave the order for the One-Horned Monster King to lead the monster kings of the seventy-two caves into battle. "I will follow with my four generals at the rear." But when the monsters reached the Iron Bridge, their path was halted by the Nine Planets.

"Make way!" Monkey shouted, brandishing his cudgel.

The Planets were quickly beaten back by Monkey's relentless attack. When they had regrouped at a safe distance, they shouted, "You witless, insensitive groomer of horses, there is no crime you have not committed! First you stole peaches and wine, then you spoiled the banquet before it started, after which you purloined Lao-tzu's immortal elixir. Not satisfied even with all that, you returned and plundered the imperial winery a second time. Don't you realize that you have added sin upon sin?"

"It's all true," Monkey said. "What are you going to do about it?"

"We have been sent by the Jade Emperor to receive your submission. If you submit at once we will spare the other creatures, but if you resist we will stamp this mountain flat and pulverize your cave until it looks like the dead ashes of yesterday's fire."

"You'd better have magic powers to back up your words," Monkey retorted. "Stand your ground if you can, and see how you like Monkey's cudgel!"

The Nine Planets mounted an attack, but they were no match for Monkey. They were soon routed. Once back in their tents, they reported to Vaishravana that they could not hold their own against the Monkey King.

Vaishravana next ordered the Kings of the Four Quarters and the Twenty-Eight Constellations to advance into battle. In turn, Monkey readied the One-Horned Monster King and the monsters of the seventy-two caves to meet the challenge. Together with Monkey and his four generals they took their stand outside the cave.

The fierce battle that ensued raged from dawn until the setting of the sun. The One-Horned Monster King and his troops were defeated and taken into captivity. Monkey's troops, along with the four generals, escaped by hiding deep inside the caves, while Monkey himself was able singlehandedly to hold off the Kings of the Four Quarters, Vaishravana, and Natha. The battle waged on through the day, with neither side gaining the advantage. Seeing that night was descending, Monkey plucked a handful of hairs from his body, chewed them into tiny pieces, and, spitting them out, cried, "Change!" They instantly became a thousand monkey demons, each brandishing a cudgel, and led by Monkey quickly forced their opponents to withdraw.

Victorious at last, Monkey withdrew his hairs and returned to the cave. He was met at the Iron Bridge by his generals and the troop of monkeys. As he flew down from the sky to greet them, they first kowtowed, then sobbed, "Oh, oh, oh," and finally laughed, "Ho, ho, ho."

"What is the meaning of this?" Monkey said.

The generals replied, "We cried because when the monsters did battle this morning they were defeated and captured. And then we laughed because you returned home victorious and unharmed."

"Victory and defeat are the common lot of all warriors," Monkey said. "There is a saying, 'To kill ten thousand you must sacrifice three thousand.' At least in this instance those captured were only wolves, tigers, elephants, leopards, and the like. Since no monkeys were injured or captured, we needn't worry. Now we must take our rest, eat, and restore our bodies, for tomorrow the battle will rage again. With my potent magic I will capture some of those generals from Heaven to avenge our comrades."

The Jade Emperor had been waiting with grave impatience for news from the front. Upon opening the memorial sent by Vaishravana and reading its contents not once, but twice, he said, "This is outrageous! We are being asked to send reinforcements. How can it be that one hundred thousand troops cannot subdue a single Monkey spirit? What do they expect me to do now?"

The Bodhisattva Kuan-yin bowed reverently and said, "Your Majesty, do not trouble yourself. If you will heed my humble recommendation, I know of one who can capture the monkey wizard."

"Who might that be?"

"Your Majesty's nephew, the illustrious sage Erh-lang, who lives at the mouth of the River of Libations, where he enjoys the incense and oblations that ascend to him from the Region Below. In the past he slew the six bogies. He has under his command the Brothers of Plum Mountain and twelve hundred straw-headed gods. His magical powers are enormous. Although he cannot be compelled to any summons to come here personally, I believe he would dispatch his troops to the scene of the battle if he were to receive an edict from Your Majesty."

The Jade Emperor immediately summoned the demon king Mahabali to present the edict. Riding his cloud, it took Mahabali less than half an hour to reach Erh-lang's temple. Incense was burned, and then the edict was read to Erh-lang and his brothers. Without hesitation Erh-lang gave his consent, saying he would help to the utmost of his powers.

Calling his six brothers together, he said, "The Jade Emperor has commanded us to journey to the Mountain of Flowers and Fruit to subdue a demon monkey." The brothers were pleased by Erh-lang's challenge and, marshalling their troops, came into formation with falcons on their wrists and bows in their hands. Leading their dogs, they rode a wild magic wind across the great Eastern Ocean. Landing on the mountain, they saw that their way was blocked by a multistranded cosmic net. Shouting their marching orders, they were soon met by Vaishravana and Prince Natha, who gave them a briefing of the military situation that faced them. Erh-lang said, "I see that I will have to engage that baneful Monkey in a contest of transformations. I will need your troops to draw the net tight around the circumference, but be sure to leave the top uncovered. Should Monkey beat me in this contest, do not come to my assistance, as my brothers will provide the only support I will need. Nor will I need you if I am victorious, for then my brothers will tie the monkey up. However, I will need Vaishravana to hold a position in midair with his imp-reflecting mirror. I'm afraid if I get the best of this simian monster he will try to flee, so it is imperative that you keep him in view at all times."

With the Heavenly troops at their stations, Erh-lang led his own troops, surrounded by his brothers, to the Water Curtain Cave. The straw-headed deities stood at the ready with their leashed dogs and hooded falcons. When Erh-lang read Monkey's banner he was outraged. "How dare this hairy fiend call himself the equal of Heaven!" he bellowed.

"Never mind that," his brothers warned. "Go forward and make the challenge."

When the monkeys outside the cave ran inside to warn Monkey that a new adversary was at the gate, Monkey at once donned his golden armor, slipped into his cloud-stepping shoes, and, giving his cap a commanding tug, marched out of the cave.

Monkey looked the long-eared monster over, from his triple-peaked phoenix cap to his dragon-coiled boots, and let out a hoot of laughter. "Whose little warrior are you, and where do you hail from?" he asked.

"If you don't know who I am, you must be blind. Either

*Great Sage, Equal of Heaven, prepares his troops
for battle.*

that or your eye sockets are bereft of their orbs. I am the nephew of the Jade Emperor. His Majesty has ordered me to arrest you. Your troublemaking days are over."

"Now it comes to me," Monkey said. "Some years ago the Jade Emperor's sister became fascinated with the Lower Regions. She fell in love with a mortal by the name of Yang and had a son by him. It was said of this boy that he cleaved the Peach Mountain with an ax. I suppose you are the foolhardy man who was once that foolish boy. You are fortunate that I have no grievance with you, else I would put an end to your sorry existence with one blow of my magic cudgel. So run along before I lose my patience. And see that you send forth the Four Great Kings."

Erh-lang was furious. "You insolent monkey!" he roared, and brought down his blade with all his might. But Monkey anticipated the blow and blocked it with his cudgel. Swirling into the air, they waged a fierce battle of three hundred blows, with neither gaining the advantage. Seeing he could not win the fight on equal terms, Erh-lang cast a magic spell, shook himself, and turned into a giant one hundred thousand feet tall. Holding a magic trident with both hands, he was blue-faced, with protruding fangs, a scarlet head, and a hideous, ferocious expression. But before he could land a single blow with his trident, Monkey had transformed himself into an exact counterpart of this demon. Instead of wielding a trident, however, Monkey held in his hand a giant cudgel that resembled one of the Heavenly supporting pillars on top of Mount K'un-lun.

Monkey's generals were so terrified by these warring monster apparitions that they began to tremble and dropped their banners. His other officers dropped their swords. At the sight of Monkey's trembling officers, the six brothers of Erh-lang gave the order and their straw-headed divinities rushed in with their dogs and falcons, capturing three thousand monsters, while all the monkeys rushed screaming up the mountain, some of them escaping into the cave.

When Monkey saw his troops scattered and his remaining monsters captured, he panicked and, resuming his original form, fled in the direction of the river, where he quickly changed himself into a fish. Erh-lang was hot on his heels, but when he reached the stream's edge Monkey had disappeared. "He's changed himself into a fish," Erh-lang thought, and he changed himself into a cormorant and began flying over the water.

Monkey looked up from his hideout in the shadow of a rock and saw a dark bird skimming the surface. He thought, "It looks like a blue kite, except that its plumage isn't blue; it looks like an egret, but it doesn't have a tuft on its head; I would say it was a crane, but its feet aren't red. Of course!— it's Erh-lang in hot pursuit." Monkey released a few bubbles and swam away.

"That fish swimming beneath the bubbles," Erh-lang thought, "looks like a carp except that its tail isn't red. I would say it was a perch, but it isn't striped; it would be a snake fish, surely, but there aren't any stars on its head; it would be a bream if only it had bristles on its gills. There's only one answer: that fish was the demon monkey." Erh-lang swooped down and snapped at Monkey with his beak, but Monkey was too quick for him; leaping out of the water, he changed into a water snake and wriggled toward shore, where he hid in the grass along the bank. When Erh-lang made his pass he saw the snake just as it reached the bank. Turning quickly, he became a scarlet-crested gray crane and, with his long pointed beak, jabbed along the grassy bank, but Monkey gave a shake and turned into a spotted bustard standing stupidly on the bank.

Erh-lang stopped in his tracks, threw his head back, and

wrinkled his nose. "Lowest and basest of birds," he said under his breath, "not caring whether you mate with phoenix, eagle, or crow, I'll not touch you with pincer, hand, or claw." So saying, he reverted to his true form, dashed off for his bow, and flew an arrow that sent the bustard flying head over hindquarters.

When Monkey came to his senses he realized he was tumbling down a steep hill. Seizing the opportunity, once he had rolled out of sight he turned himself into a wayside shrine. He transformed his mouth into the entrance and his teeth into doors; his tongue was a bodhisattva, and his eyes became windows. Not knowing what to do with his tail, he stuck it straight up and changed it into a flagpole.

When Erh-lang reached the bottom of the hill, instead of a bustard he saw a small shrine. He examined its features carefully, and noticing the flagpole, he laughed. "So it's Monkey again, up to his old tricks. I've seen countless shrines before, but never one with a flagpole sticking up in back! This is another one of his animal-transforming tricks. He's trying to lure me inside so he can bite me. Instead I'll smash his windows and kick down his doors."

When Monkey overheard Erh-lang, he thought, "Those are my eyes and teeth he's talking about." At once he turned himself into a tiger and leaped out of sight.

Erh-lang was suddenly standing on the bank before a vanished shrine, shaking his head, when his brothers arrived. He explained the situation and then said, "Brothers, keep a lookout for him down here, and I'll search for him above." Ascending a cloud, Erh-lang soon came to Vaishravana, who was dutifully holding his imp-detecting mirror. "Have you seen that foul Monkey?" Erh-lang asked.

"He's not been up here," Vaishravana replied. "I've been watching with my mirror, you know."

When Erh-lang explained in detail all that had transpired, Vaishravana listened carefully, flipped his mirror completely around, and suddenly exclaimed, "Quick! Quick! That Monkey has made himself invisible! He's slipped through the magic cordon and is heading straight for the River of Libations."

When Monkey arrived at the river, he changed into the form of Erh-lang and went straight to the latter's temple. The demon guardians kowtowed before Monkey, thinking he was their master. He took his seat in the middle of the temple and began to accept the various offerings that were brought to him. Suddenly a report rang through the chambers. "Another Erh-lang has arrived." The various demon magistrates rushed out to have a look and were thunderstruck at the sight of the real Erh-lang. "I see by your faces," he said, "that the Great Sage, Equal of Heaven, has arrived at our temple."

"We've not seen such a being as that," they cried, "but there is another Erh-lang inside, seated on the throne."

Erh-lang crashed through the door and confronted Monkey, who instantly resumed his natural form. "Calm down," Monkey said, "this temple now belongs to me."

"This time you've gone too far," Erh-lang shouted, and he raised his trident and aimed a blow at Monkey's head. Monkey dodged out of the way, took the needle from behind his ear, which instantly became a cudgel. Slashing and cursing, the two adversaries fought their way out of the temple and continued the battle all the way back to the Mountain of Flowers and Fruit, where Erh-lang was met by the Four Kings and his six brothers; together they quickly surrounded Monkey on all sides.

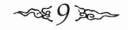

In the Buddha's Palm

*T*HE Jade Emperor had once again grown uneasy. An entire day had passed, and there was still no news from Erh-lang and his battalions. Seeing the troubled state of the Jade Emperor, Kuan-yin said, "With Your Majesty's permission, Lao-tzu and I would like to see for ourselves how the battle is going." The Jade Emperor consented, and together they went to the Southern Gate of Heaven to have a look.

When they opened the gate and peered down, they could see the cosmic nets that were being manned on every side, as well as Vaishravana with his imp-reflecting mirror. Then they spotted Monkey and Erh-lang far, far below, engaged in fierce combat. Kuan-yin said, "My choice of Erh-lang was a good one. He has magic powers, and he is holding his own with Monkey. With just a little help from above he will be able to achieve his end."

"What do you propose?" Lao-tzu asked.

"I'll throw down my immaculate vase. When it hits Monkey it will throw him off balance, and that will be enough to enable Erh-lang to make the capture."

"Your vase is made of porcelain," Lao-tzu said. "If it hits him on the head it will go as you say, but should it fall on his iron cudgel it will be shattered."

"Have you a better plan?" the Jade Emperor asked Lao-tzu.

Lao-tzu rolled up his sleeve and pulled down an armlet. "This weapon of red steel has been compounded by a magic

74

elixir that I made myself; this imbues it with supernatural force. It has transformational powers and is impervious to the effects of fire and water. It can be used, among other things, as a snare." Without another word, Lao-tzu flung it down, and they watched intently as it billowed out and slowly floated down over Monkey's head.

Monkey was immediately thrown off his feet by the snare. He tried to stumble away, but Erh-lang's dogs were close on his heels and caused him to lose his balance and become entangled in the netting. With the brothers holding him down, Erh-lang bound him tight with ropes and severed his lute-bone, so he could no longer transform himself.

When all the forces had gathered around Erh-lang to pay homage to his great victory, he deferred their compliments, saying, "This is all the result of the Heavenly contingents and proper exercise of divine authority. I can take no credit."

The brothers said, "What we should do now is take this villain up to Heaven and see how the Jade Emperor wishes to dispose of him."

"My good brothers," Erh-lang said, "only those with a divine appointment may have an audience with His Presence. The Heavenly soldiers will hoist him up, while Vaishravana and I go up to make our report. After you've combed the mountain and have seen that everything is in order, return to the River of Libations. Once we have recorded our deeds and I have received my reward, I shall return to you and we will have a grand celebration."

Erh-lang led the triumphant march to Heaven, with songs of victory being sung on the way. When they reached the Hall of Perfect Light their report was memorialized to the Throne. "The Heavenly Squadrons led by Erh-lang have captured the monstrous monkey Great Sage, Equal of Heaven, and await the order of Your Majesty."

75

The Jade Emperor then commanded that the demon king Mahabali and a contingent of Heavenly troops march Monkey to the monster execution block, where he would be cut into small pieces.

Monkey was brought to the place of execution and bound to the demon-subduing pillar. The executioners slashed at him with spears, but they were unable to harm his body. The Southern Pole Star ordered the fire agents to set him afire, but this too did no good. Next the gods of thunder were ordered to strike him with thunderbolts, but this also had no effect. Neither fire nor the thunderbolts were able to singe even a single hair on the body of Monkey.

Mahabali returned to the Throne and reported to the Jade Emperor, "Your Majesty, that baneful Monkey has proven himself to be inviolable. We've hacked, hewed, and slashed at him with sword, ax, and spears; neither this nor fire and thunderbolts have had the least effect. What are we to do?"

"I see," the Jade Emperor said. "To capture him is one thing, to kill him is another."

Lao-tzu stepped forward. "It is not surprising," he said. "We do not know what powers Monkey arrived with in Heaven, but we do know that while he was here he ate of the immortal peaches, drank the Imperial wine, and even, further, gobbled up five potfuls of my divine elixir. These ingredients have no doubt been refined in his stomach by the Samadhi fire, giving his body a diamondlike indestructibility. That's my guess. If I could take him to my alchemical laboratory and place him in the Crucible of Eight Trigrams and smelt him with the alchemical fires, he would soon be reduced to ash. In this way we would have the dead ashes of Monkey and I would be able to recover my elixir, which would be left at the bottom of the crucible."

Monkey was released into Lao-tzu's custody by the

Twelve Guardians of Light and Darkness. In the meantime Erh-lang was rewarded with a hundred golden flowers, a hundred bottles of Imperial wine, and a hundred pills of elixir, together with rare jewels, embroideries, and other treasures that he was to share with his brothers upon his return to the River of Libations.

When Lao-tzu returned to the Tushita Palace with Monkey in tow, he first untied his knots and then removed the blade that still was struck through Monkey's lute-bone. Pushing him into the crucible, he ordered his servants to stoke up a good fire. Monkey well knew that the crucible was comprised of eight compartments representing the Eight Trigrams. Thus once inside the crucible he crawled into the compartment corresponding to the Sun Trigram. Sun symbolizes wind, and Monkey knew that where there is wind there is no fire. However, wind blowing through fire churns up smoke. Hence the smoke in the crucible immediately reddened Monkey's eyes, a condition from which he never recovered. It was from this experience that he later earned the nickname Fiery Eyes.

At last the forty-ninth day arrived, and the alchemical process that would reduce Monkey to ashes was completed. When Lao-tzu lifted the lid he looked down in amazement to see Monkey, still whole and complete, rubbing his eyes with both hands, tears streaming down his cheeks. Monkey was startled by the sudden light, which stabbed at his already red and swollen eyes. He leapt out with such force that the crucible fell over, making a loud crash. He raced out of the laboratory with Lao-tzu and the servants chasing behind. When Lao-tzu clutched at Monkey's sleeve he was given a shove that sent him sprawling head over heels. Monkey then took the needle from behind his ear, instantly transformed it into an iron cudgel, and went rampaging through Heaven.

With Monkey out of control, the Nine Planets shut themselves up and the Four Heavenly Kings simply disappeared from sight. Monkey slashed his way through the Hall of Perfect Light and was approaching the Treasure Hall of Divine Mists when he was challenged by the divinity Wang Ling-kuan, who held him off with his golden mace while he sent word to the Thunder Palace to send thirty-six thunder deities to engage Monkey in battle. Monkey was soon surrounded by the deities, who thundered and crashed all around him, wielding their spears, lances, swords, halberds, whips, maces, hammers, axes, sickles, spades, scimitars, hooks, and the like. Just as Monkey was about to be cornered, he cast a magic spell, shook himself, and turned into a monster with six arms and three heads, wielding six magic cudgels. Whirring like a spinning wheel, dancing and jigging, he made himself unapproachable.

The noise of the battle soon reached the Jade Emperor, who at once sent an envoy to the Western Region to ask for the Buddha's help. After the Buddha had been given a full report of Monkey's history in Heaven, his evil deeds, and his corruptible yet indomitable spirit, the Buddha, without any expression of dismay, said to the various bodhisattvas in his court, "Do not stir from here, but keep your bearing correct while in the Dharma Hall, and do not relax your meditation postures. I will soon return, after I have exorcised a demon and defended the Throne." Accompanied by his venerable disciples, Ananda and Kashyapa, he left the Thunderclap Temple and soon arrived at the Treasure Hall of Divine Mists, where they were met by the deafening noise of an ongoing battle between Monkey and the thunderbolts. The Buddha at once ordered the thirty-six thunder deities to lower their arms and return to their camp. He then ordered Monkey to appear before him to explain his magic powers.

Monkey resumed his natural form and came forward, shouting angrily, "Who are you, old monk, to stop our battle and give me a direct order?"

The Buddha laughed. "I am the Venerable One from the Western Region of Perfect Bliss. I have received a full report of your rebellious behavior since coming to Heaven. I would like to know where you were born, how you received your magic, and why you have been so unruly."

"I hail from the Mountain of Flowers and Fruit, where I have reigned as the Handsome Monkey King. Born of Heaven and Earth, I wandered until I found a friend and master who taught me the Great Mystery, and I am now an immortal. When I grew tired of the restricted life of humans, I came to Heaven determined to live in the Green Jade Sky. Why should Heaven have but one master, when on Earth king follows king? If might is honor, then none are mightier than I, or more honorable. This is why I dare to fight, for only heroes deserve to win and rule."

The Buddha laughed again, but scornfully. "You are only a monkey who by chance became an immortal spirit. What effrontery to presume that you could seize the throne of His Presence the Jade Emperor! He has been perfecting himself for 1,750 kalpas, with each kalpa lasting 129,000 years. And you deign to compare your wisdom with his! Why, you are nothing but a beast who has—however miraculously—attained a humanlike form solely in this incarnation. You commit blasphemy by talking in this way, and this can only lead to the shortening of your allotted age. Repent at once, or I will put an end to you, and whatever of value you have achieved will be wasted."

Monkey looked the Buddha up and down before he spoke. "It doesn't matter to me how long the Jade Emperor has been practicing religion. Why should this give him longevity on the throne? As the proverb says, 'Emperors come in their turn, next year the turn shall be mine.' Tell him to move over and make room for Monkey, and that will be the end of the matter. If he refuses, there will be no peace in Heaven."

"Tell me," the Buddha said, "besides your immortality and your transforming magic, what powers do you possess to enable you to conquer and usurp the blessed and hallowed realms of Heaven?"

"In addition to seventy-two transformations, I will not grow old for ten thousand kalpas. In addition, I can somersault above the clouds and with one leap travel eight thousand miles. Are you to tell me that I am not qualified to sit on the throne of Heaven?"

"Since we have come to a difference on this matter," the Buddha said in a conciliatory tone, "I would like to make you a wager. If you can leap off the palm of my right hand, I will ask the Jade Emperor to come and live with me in the West and give you his throne. But if you cannot leap out of my hand, you must return to the Lower Regions and become one of the monsters, where you must work through a few more kalpas before you will be able to return to Heaven and speak to me again."

Monkey snickered and said to himself, "This Buddha is a fool. With a single somersault I can travel eight thousand miles, and the palm of his hand is scarcely eight inches across." He looked up at the Buddha. "Are you certain that your decision will stand up?"

"Of course I am," the Buddha replied, stretching out his hand, which was about the size of a lotus leaf. Monkey reduced his cudgel to a needle, slipped it behind his ear, and, leaping onto the Buddha's hand, shouted, "I'm off!" He bounded away like a streak of lightning. But the Buddha, watching him with the trained eye of wisdom, looked down and saw a whirligig cast in a spin.

Monkey had been sailing along for some time when he saw in the distance five flesh-colored pillars standing straight up in the sky. "This must be the end of the line," he thought. "When I get back the Buddha will be my witness and the Palace of Divine Mists will be mine." But just as he was starting to turn around he had another thought. "Wait a minute!" he declared to himself. "Shouldn't I leave some evidence, just in case the Buddha doesn't believe me?" He plucked a hair from his body and blew on it with his magic breath, saying, "Change!" It instantly became a writing brush charged with heavy ink. Walking to the central pillar, he wrote, "The Great Sage, Equal of Heaven, was here!" And then, in utter disrespect, he pissed against the base of the pillar.

When Monkey had somersaulted back and was standing again on Buddha's palm, he cocked his hat and said, "Well, I took my little journey, and now I'm back. You can tell the Jade Emperor to vacate his palace."

"Why, you stinking baboon, you never once left the palm of my hand."

"Don't display your ignorance," said Monkey. "I went to the farthest reaches of Heaven, and when I found five flesh-colored pillars I left my mark on the middle pillar. Would you care to go out with me and have a look?"

"No need," the Buddha answered. "Just drop your head and have a look yourself." Monkey peered down, and there, scrawled on the middle finger of the Buddha, was written "The Great Sage, Equal of Heaven, was here!" At that moment he caught a whiff of monkey urine coming from the fork between the Buddha's thumb and first finger.

Monkey refused to believe his eyes. "This can't be! This

Monkey approaches the five pillars

at the farthest reaches of Heaven.

can't be! I wrote those words on a pillar supporting the sky. So how did those words get here? It must be a dirty trick of divination. This can't be happening to me. I'll go back for another look." Monkey was about to crouch for another leap when the Buddha flipped his hand over and sent Monkey sailing out the West Heavenly Gate, and as he did so he transformed his five fingers into the Five Elements, metal, wood, water, fire, and earth, which instantly became the Mountain of Five Elements, pinning Monkey to the ground with enough pressure to hold him securely in place.

The thunder spirits, Ananda, and Kashyapa put their palms together to praise the Buddha. "Wonderful! Wonderful!" they chanted. "But look, the Great Sage is sticking out his head."

"Not to worry," the Buddha said, and took out from his sleeve an engraving stamped in gold letters, which read OM MANI PADME HUM. Handing it to Ananda, he told him to stamp it on top of the mountain. When this was done the mountain immediately struck root and grew together at the seams. Monkey was left with breathing space only and just enough squeezing room for his head and hands to move.

Before saying good-bye to the Jade Emperor and all the spirits, the Buddha approached a guardian spirit and the Fearless Guards of Five Quarters and told them to stand watch over the mountain. He gave them instructions to feed Monkey iron pills when he was hungry and to give him molten verdigris to drink when he was thirsty. "When the days of his punishment are complete," the Buddha declared, "someone will come to rescue him."

10

Kuan-yin's Search for a Pilgrim

*T*HE Buddha was seated on his Lotus Throne, lecturing to his congregation. At the close of his formal talk, he said to the bodhisattvas and arhats who were still in attendance, "I have noticed a great variance in the morality of the inhabitants of the Four Continents of the universe. Those in the Eastern Continent are straightforward, upright, and peaceful. Those in the Northern Continent will kill other living creatures for their food, but they are dull-witted and lethargic in spirit, so they don't do much harm. Those in the Western Continent neither covet nor slaughter, and although none are illuminated they are even-tempered and rational and live to a ripe old age. But in the Southern Continent they are greedy and lustful, treacherous and murderous, and assuredly full of malice and spite.

Buddha paused and took in the congregation. "It is fortunate for us all that I am in possession of three bundles of scriptures that could influence the people of the Southern Continent."

When the Buddha's disciples heard these words they pressed their palms together and, touching their foreheads, bowed before their Master. "Which of the authentic scriptures are these?" they asked.

"The bundle called Vinaya speaks of Heaven, the bundle entitled Shastras tells of the Earth, while the third bundle, the Sutras, can redeem the damned. Altogether these scriptures consist of thirty-five scrolls. They are the scriptures for the cultivation of truth and lead to the gate of perfection. I would send these to the Eastern lands if the inhabitants were not so stupid and corruptible. They do not understand the meaning of the Law and are scornful of the true sect of Yoga.

"There is only one way for us to save the people of the Eastern lands. One of us must journey there to seek and find a virtuous believer. We need someone who is willing to endure the travails of traveling over a thousand mountains, across ten thousand bodies of water, in quest of those authentic scriptures that once implanted in the East will enlighten the people and deliver them from darkness. If one of us were to go there and find a true believer who would travel here, I would turn over the scriptures. Which of you will go in search of such a one to carry out this task?"

The Bodhisattva Kuan-yin made her way to the lotus platform. She bowed three times to the Buddha before speaking. "Although I am unqualified and unworthy," she said, "I would like to go to the Land of the East in search of a pilgrim for the scriptures."

"No one is better qualified and more perfectly suited for this task than the venerable Bodhisattva," the Buddha said.

Kuan-yin asked, "Have you any instructions for me before I depart?"

"As you travel," the Buddha replied, "you must study the path very carefully. Do not travel with the stars, but keep a low altitude, between mist and cloud, so as to have an exact record of the distances between mountains and waterways. It is important that our pilgrim have an accurate description of the land he will be journeying over. Even so the pilgrim's journey will be hard, and so I have prepared five talismans that you are to give him." The Buddha then ordered Ananda and Kashyapa to bring forward an embroidered cassock and a priestly staff of nine rings. "When you present these to the pilgrim, tell him that the cassock will strengthen his resolve during moments of weakness. The staff will ward off negativity and violence."

The Bodhisattva received the first two talismans and bowed before the Buddha, who then spoke further. "Here also is a headband. Should the pilgrim meet with any monster possessing magic powers who wishes to be a disciple of the pilgrim but who may from time to time prove wicked or unruly, the pilgrim is to place this band around his disciple's head. Then whenever he recites the spell belonging to that headband it will cause such pain to the monster that he will easily be persuaded to obey the pilgrim."

Kuan-yin set off on the journey with her disciple Hui-an at her side. Acting as her bodyguard, Hui-an carried a great iron cudgel weighing one thousand pounds. Kuan-yin made a bundle of the cassock and carried it on her back. The headband she stuffed up her sleeve, and the nine-ringed staff she carried in her hand.

They had not traveled far when they came to a large body of water called the River of Flowing Sands. "My disciple," the Bodhisattva said, "this will be a very difficult body of water to cross for one of mortal flesh and bone. How can it be done?"

Hui-an said, "We need first to know just how great a body of water this is." Kuan-yin went forward on her cloud to have a look when there was a sudden splash and out leaped a hideous monster. He came thrashing through the waves waving his staff in the air and pointed it at the Bodhisattva. Hui-an cried, "Halt!" and went flying after the monster, brandishing his iron cudgel. A fierce battle ensued, with neither monster

靈感大王
れいかんだいおう

*The Bodhisattva Kuan-yin with her
disciple and bodyguard, Hui-an*

nor disciple able to gain the advantage. When they had gone thirty rounds without a decision, the monster stopped, held up his iron staff in defense, and said, "What is the name of the monk who dares oppose me?"

"The disciple Hui-an is Moksha, the second son of the Pagoda Bearer Vaishravana. My mentor is seeking a scripture pilgrim from the Land of the East, and I am her guardian. What kind of evil spirit are you that dares to stand in her way?"

"Now I remember," the monster said. "I used to see you in the bamboo grove of the Southern Ocean practicing austerities under the guidance of Kuan-yin. But where is the Bodhisattva?"

"She is over there, on the shore. Don't you recognize her?" The monster turned crimson. Bowing his obeisance, he laid down his staff and allowed Hui-an to bring him before Kuan-yin. "I beg the Bodhisattva's forgiveness. You see, I am no monster at all but the Curtain-Raising Marshal who used to wait upon the phoenix chariot of the Jade Emperor at the Treasure Hall of Divine Mists. At one of the Heavenly banquets I carelessly broke a crystal cup, and for this the Jade Emperor ordered that I receive eight hundred lashes. He banished me to the Region Below and cast me into my present shape. Every seventh day a flying sword is sent to stab my chest and side more than one hundred times. But that is not all. I am always cold and hungry, and have only my own company to keep. Every few days, when I can bear it no longer, I come out of hiding and find a traveler to eat. I had no idea that the traveler I attempted to feed on today was none other than the venerable Bodhisattva Kuan-yin."

"You are here because of your sin in Heaven," said Kuan-yin, "but now you are taking lives. By your conduct you are adding sin to sin. By official decree I am journeying to the

Land of the East to search for a scripture pilgrim. If you will reform your ways and join our sect and become a disciple of the scripture pilgrim and go with him to receive the scriptures from the Buddha, I will see that the flying swords no longer pierce you. If the expedition is a success, your sin will be forgiven, and you will be able to return to your old position. How does that sound?"

"I have a confession to make," the monster said in reply. "Among the humans I have devoured have been a number of scripture pilgrims, nine in all. If you ask how I know with certainty that there were precisely nine, I will tell you that it is the nature of this water that not even goose down will float upon it. And yet the skulls of those nine pilgrims will not sink. One day I threaded the skulls together, and now, from time to time, I use them for sport. I'm afraid that if your scripture pilgrim were to hear of this, he would not come this way, and therefore I cannot be saved."

"On the contrary," the Bodhisattva replied, "not only will the pilgrim come this way, but he will find a good use for them. Hang them around your neck and take your vows."

The monster was ordained the Sandy Priest, after the region in which he was serving penance. After the Bodhisattva had given him the commandments and departed, the Sandy Priest—or Sandy, as he would thereafter be called—washed his heart and purified himself. From that time on he took not a single life, but instead waited faithfully for the arrival of the scripture pilgrim.

The Bodhisattva and her disciple then took their departure from the Sandy Priest and continued their journey. They soon came to a mountain infected with a miasma so foul that they were stopped dead in their tracks. They were about to ascend a cloud when a mad blast of wind brought into view another monster of ferocious appearance. His ears looked like rush-leaf fans, and his drooping lips curled into a snarl. He came whirling out of the wind straight in their direction and, brandishing his muckrake, made a strike at the Bodhisattva. Hui-an blocked the demon's weapon with his cudgel, and cried, "Hideous monster, watch your manners and look out for my cudgel!"

"Foolish monk," the monster shouted back, "don't you know when you are outclassed? Back off at once or I'll put an end to your indolence and your life with a single blow."

With that exchange the battle began. To the monster's surprise, the young disciple was his equal in valor and strength. Kuan-yin, who was watching the fight from her cloud, threw down a handful of lotus flowers to separate the clashing weapons. "What kind of warrior are you," the monster cried, "that you dare play the trick on me of Flower-in-the-eye?"

"Cursed monster," Hui-an cried, "I am the disciple of the Bodhisattva Kuan-yin, and it was she that threw down the flowers."

"You don't mean the Bodhisattva from the Southern Ocean! Not Kuan-yin herself, who saves us from the Three Calamities and rescues us from the Eight Disasters."

"I mean none other."

The monster threw down his muckrake and, lowering his head, said, "Elder Brother, where is the Bodhisattva? Please present me to her."

Hui-an pointed upward. "There she is," he said. The monster fiend kowtowed and cried at the top of his voice, "Forgive me, Bodhisattva, forgive me!"

Kuan-yin lowered her cloud and addressed the monster. "What are you, a wild boar turned devil, or just a tame old sow who has become a fiend?"

"I am neither one," the monster answered. "I used to be the Marshal of the Heavenly Reeds in the Heavenly River.

One day I got a little drunk and became cozy with the Goddess of the Moon. For this the Jade Emperor had me beaten two thousand times with a mallet and then banished me to the Lower Regions. Seeking a correct home for my next incarnation, I lost my way and mistakenly entered the womb of an old sow. That accounts for my looks. When I came to my senses I bit the sow to death and killed the rest of the litter. Since then I've been wandering over this mountain range, eating people and passing my days. How could I know that I would run into the Bodhisattva one day? I implore you, please save me!"

"There is an old proverb, 'If you want to have a future, act with reverence toward the future.' You have not repented for your transgressions in Heaven. And by living on human flesh in the World Below you are setting yourself up for a double punishment."

The harsh words of Kuan-yin caused the monster to lose his temper. "Don't talk to me about the future!" he said. "The future, indeed! According to you I should live on air. The proverb says, 'If you follow the law of the land you'll be flogged to death; if you follow the law of the Buddhists you'll starve to death.' Leave me be! What interests me is eating a traveler or two, and when I'm lucky some plump, juicy maiden. What do I care about double-sinning, triple-sinning, or sinning a thousand times?"

"There is a saying, 'Heaven helps those who help themselves.' Everything will change for the good, if only you will turn toward the good. There are five kinds of grain in the world, and each relieves hunger. You do not need to feed on humans in order to live."

The monster shook himself, as if waking from a dream. "I would like to follow the path of truth, but now that I have sinned against Heaven, can there be any hope for me?"

"It is never too late," the Bodhisattva said. "At the Buddha's decree we are traveling to the Land of the East in search of a scripture pilgrim. If, when the pilgrim passes this way, you were to follow him as a disciple to the Western Heaven, you will atone for your sins by your own merits, and in this way you will be delivered from your earthly incarnation."

"Oh, I will, I will," the monster cried. The Bodhisattva laid her hands on his head and administered the vows. "From now on your religious name will be Pigsy. You are to fast, do penance for your past sins, and wait faithfully for the pilgrim."

❧

The Bodhisattva and her disciple had not gone far when they came upon a dragon suspended in midair. "What dragon are you?" Kuan-yin enquired, "and why have you been removed from your natural environment?"

"I am the son of Ao-jun, the Dragon King of the Western Ocean. I inadvertently set fire to his palace, and some of his precious magic pearls were destroyed. My father reported me to the Heavenly Court, calling it an act of rebellion. The Jade Emperor hung me in the sky and gave me three hundred lashes. I shall be executed any day now. I beg the Bodhisattva to save me!"

Kuan-yin rushed off to Heaven. There she was met by the Divine Preceptors, who arranged an audience with the Jade Emperor. After explaining the nature of her mission, the Bodhisattva said to the Jade Emperor, "I beg you to spare the life of that naughty dragon hanging in the sky. If you will turn him over to me I will be able to use him in my mission for the Buddha."

The Jade Emperor willingly gave permission, and the Bodhisattva, with her disciple at her side, rode back on her cloud. She ordered the dragon to retire to a deep ravine. "When the pilgrim arrives you are to turn into a white horse in the service of the scripture pilgrim."

The Bodhisattva and her disciple continued on their journey. On the following day they were suddenly aware of ten thousand shafts of golden light and a thousand wreaths of radiant vapor. "Teacher," Hui-an said, "that is the Mountain of Five Elements. I can see the imprint of Buddha's seal upon it. Isn't that the mountain where the Great Sage, Equal of Heaven, is imprisoned? The one who upset the Peach Banquet and threw the Heavenly Palace into chaos?"'

"That's correct," the Bodhisattva replied. They ascended the mountain together and read the seal: OM MANI PADME HUM. Suddenly they heard a voice rising up from the base of the mountain. "Who is that up there, trampling on my mountain and reciting my misdeeds?"

The Bodhisattva and Hui-an started down toward the voice and were met by the Heavenly Sentinels. They came and bowed before the Bodhisattva and led her to the Great Sage. He was imprisoned in an iron box, and although he could speak he could not move his body. "Do you recognize me, Monkey?" the Bodhisattva asked.

Monkey peered at her with his fiery eyes. "Of course I recognize you. You are the All-compassionate, All-merciful Bodhisattva Kuan-yin from the Potalaka Mountain of the Southern Ocean. Thank mercy you've come to see me. I have never been visited before, and every day here is like a year. Why have you come?"

"I am traveling at the Buddha's decree to the Land of the East to find a scripture pilgrim. Since I was passing this way, I thought I'd stop and see you."

"The Buddha tricked me," Monkey cried, "and I've been

imprisoned in this mountain for five hundred years. Show a little mercy and rescue me."

"I don't know," the Bodhisattva answered. "Your sins were very great, and I could never be sure that once you were free you wouldn't carry on as before."

"I have repented," Monkey said. "I have no other wish but to walk the straight and narrow. I want only to cultivate my conduct and practice good works."

The Bodhisattva was very pleased, and took Monkey at his word. "I will help you, but you must wait here until I find the scripture pilgrim. When you become his disciple, and by observing and upholding the faith, you will enter again the Gates of Heaven. Are you willing? Can you do that?"

"Oh, I'm willing, I'm willing!" Monkey pleaded.

"In that case, I will need to give you a religious name."

"I already have a name," Monkey said. "I'm called Aware-of-Vacuity."

"An auspicious name," the Bodhisattva said. After instructing Monkey again to wait for the pilgrim, they continued their journey eastward.

In a few days they reached Ch'ang-an, the capital city of the Great T'ang Nation. Leaving their cloud, they changed themselves into shabby, wandering monks and entered the city. When they came to a temple of the local deity they went inside; there the Bodhisattva was recognized at once. After the various guardians and spirits had all kowtowed before the Bodhisattva, she said, "It must not get out that I am here. I am traveling at the Buddha's decree, in search of a pilgrim to carry the holy scriptures to China. I should like to stay in one of your temples for a few days until the true monk has been found."

11

The Journey to the West

*I*N the day of the Bodhisattva's arrival in Ch'ang-an, the Emperor had chosen the priest Hsuan-tsang to be the Supreme Commander of all priests and in all matters of religion throughout the land. Presenting Hsuan-tsang with a cassock of brocade and a Buddha visage cap, he told him to return to his temple and select a propitious day for the ceremony.

Kuan-yin, continuing her search for the right pilgrim, had remained incognito. One day she gathered up the sacred relics the Buddha had presented her with—the embroidered cassock and the nine-ringed staff—and with her disciple went out into the streets. When they reached the Eastern Flower Gate, they met the chief minister, Hsiao Yu, who was returning from Court. His outriders were clearing the streets, but Kuan-yin refused to step aside. Standing in the middle of the street, she held up the cassock and effectively blocked the minister's path. He reined in his horse, clearly dazzled by this embroidered cassock that was so different from any he had seen before. He told one of his servants to ascertain the price.

"Twelve thousand gold coins for the cassock," said the Bodhisattva, "and five thousand gold coins for the staff."

The minister came forward and spoke. "What makes them so expensive?"

"This cassock," said the Bodhisattva, "has something good about it, and then again it has something bad about it as well. For some people it is very expensive, for others there is no cost at all."

"What do you mean?" Hsiao Yu asked.

"The one who wears this cassock," said the Bodhisattva, "will not fall into Hell or suffer any violent harm, and he will not be attacked by wild monsters. But this is true only for the good man. If it is worn by a lustful man who indulges in iniquities, who obeys neither the dietary laws nor the commandments, why, such a one will not even be allowed to lay eyes on this cassock."

"But what do you mean, it will be expensive for some, but for others free?"

"As I said, for the unworthy one the cost is steep, but for the one who is worthy the cassock and staff will be given simply for the asking."

Hsiao-yu dismounted and bowed before the Bodhisattva, for he understood clearly now that he was speaking to a devout person. "Your Eminence," he said, "please forgive any offense I may have caused you. Our great Emperor is a man of right conduct, as are all his ministers. He is presently conducting a great service, and this cassock would be most appropriate for Hsuan-tsang, the supreme commander of the priestly order. If you will accompany me to the Throne we will have an audience with the Emperor."

The Emperor was very pleased with the generous offer. He could see with his own eyes that these were no ordinary objects that were being offered. He called Hsuan-tsang, who just then had been leading the monks in the chanting of sutras. When the cassock was draped over his shoulder and the staff placed in his hand, he looked like a true child of the Buddha.

Time passed, and the day of the final ceremonies was at hand, at which Hsuan-tsang was to deliver the final sermon.

"This is the day of the Great Ceremony," Kuan-yin told her disciple, "this being the first of seven such occasions. Let us mingle with the crowd to see how the mass is going, and find out for ourselves if this priest is worthy of my treasures. I would also like to know what division of Buddhism he is teaching."

The lofty temple resounded with divine music and Buddhist chants. Hsuan-tsang of the Great Law sat in illuminated silence on a high dais. The Bodhisattva alone was aware of all the redeemed souls who had entered these holy chambers unseen by the well-born one who had come to hear the Law, while the latter reflected that pious thoughts among humans are as plentiful as raindrops on red blossoms.

Hsuan-tsang first read the Sutra for the Salvation of the Dead, followed by Divine Protection for the Nation, and concluded his reading with an Exhortation on Right Conduct. The Bodhisattva approached the dais and called up to Hsuan-tsang, "Why are you confining yourself to the teachings of the Little Vehicle? Don't you know anything from the Great Vehicle?"

The words of the Bodhisattva filled Hsuan-tsang with wonder and delight. He leaped down from the dais and, approaching Kuan-yin, said, "Venerable Teacher, please forgive me for not realizing that there was one of such learning in our midst. It is true, none of us have any knowledge of the Great Vehicle. We are able to expound only from the Little Vehicle."

"The doctrine of the Little Vehicle," Kuan-yin said, "cannot save the souls of the dead; it rather leads only to confusion and misapprehension. I have in my possession three sections of the Great Vehicle, called the Tripitaka, or Three Bundles. With this teaching the souls of the dead can be sent to Heaven; the afflicted will be delivered from their sufferings and prolong their existence, and also they will be able to break the chain of Samsara."

As they were talking, one of the officials of the temple rushed over to the T'ang Emperor, exclaiming, "The Master of the Law was just now expounding from the Little Vehicle when two miserable mendicants called him down from the dais and began engaging him in nonsensical talk." The Emperor ordered them to be brought before him in the rear hall of the monastery. When Kuan-yin appeared before the Emperor, she neither bowed nor raised her hands in obeisance. "What does Your Majesty want of me?" she asked.

Having recognized her from the previous meeting, the Emperor asked, "Aren't you the monk that gave us the cassock the other day?"

"I am that person."

"You had a perfect right to come here, of course," the Emperor said, "to listen to the sermon and have a bowl of food, but you had no right to cause a disturbance and delay the service."

"Your Master was preaching from the Little Vehicle, which is incapable of saving the souls of the dead. We are in possession of the Tripitaka, the Great Vehicle Law of Buddha, which can save the dead, succour the afflicted, and create the indestructible body."

The Emperor was overjoyed. "Where do you keep this Great Vehicle?"

"It is located in India, where the Buddha dwells, in the Great Temple of Thunderclap of the Great Western Heaven."

"Have you memorized any portion of it?"

"Certainly," Kuan-yin answered.

The Emperor insisted that Kuan-yin climb the platform and begin a lecture at once. With her disciple, Kuan-yin rose up to the platform and then, in a single bound, soared into the air, and shaking herself, she revealed her true nature, while she held the willow spray and the sacred vase, with Moksha standing on her left, holding the staff.

The Emperor and his court were overcome and, prostrating themselves, bowed before Her Eminence. His ministers burnt incense and knelt beside their Emperor. The entire hall of priests, nuns, scholars, craftsmen, merchants, all bowed down, chanting, "Dear Bodhisattva, dear Bodhisattva."

When the Emperor had recovered himself he began to make plans to send a traveler to India to procure the Holy Scriptures. Hardly had the call gone out when the Master of the Law, Hsuan-tsang, came forward and declared his willingness to make the journey. Prostrating himself before the Emperor, he said, "Your humble monk, however unworthy, will devote himself to the seeking of the true scriptures, knowing that once they are in our possession the empire of our Lord will be eternally secured."

The Emperor was pleased. He placed his hands on Hsuan-tsang's shoulders, lifting him to his feet. "If the Master is willing to perform this great service as an expression of loyalty, undaunted by the length of the journey, the many mountains and waterways to be crossed, then I am willing to become his bond brother."

Hsuan-tsang bowed again and touched his forehead to the ground to express his gratitude. Being a truthful and righteous man, the Emperor went before the presence of the Buddha's image in the temple and bowed to Hsuan-tsang four times, addressing him as "Holy Monk, my younger brother."

Hsuan-tsang said, "Your Heavenly Grace, I am unworthy of such affection, but I can promise you that I would rather die than not attain my goal and return with the true scriptures. Hsuan-tsang then burned incense before the Buddha and made his vow.

Early the next morning, while in Court, the Emperor

signed a formal rescript authorizing Hsuan-tsang's mission and stamped it with the seal of free passage. The Imperial Board of Astronomers announced that the positions of the planets were especially favorable for a long journey.

The Emperor summoned Hsuan-tsang to the Treasure Hall and said, "My brother, this is an auspicious day for your journey, and everything has been made ready. Here are your papers and a golden bowl to collect alms. Two attendants have been selected to accompany you, and I have chosen an imperial horse for you to ride. It is saddled and packed." The Emperor then sent a servant to bring wine, and asked his bond brother if he had a byname. "Since I am a priest," Hsuan-tsang said, "I have not thought it proper to take one."

The Emperor said, "The Bodhisattva told us that the scriptures are referred to in India as the Tripitaka. Would this not be a good name for you?"

Hsuan-tsang accepted the name with thanks, but when the Emperor raised his wine glass in a parting toast, Hsuan-tsang said, "Abstinence from wine is the first prohibition of priesthood."

"Given the nature of this journey, we can make an exception." Hsuan-tsang could not refuse the Emperor, but before he could bring the cup to his lips, the Emperor scooped up a handful of dirt, ground it in his hand, and sifted it into Hsuan-tsang's glass.

When Hsuan-tsang looked puzzled, the Emperor laughed, saying, "Tell me, brother, how long will it be before you return home?"

"I hope to be back in three years' time," Hsuan-tsang answered.

"That's a long time," the Emperor said, "and the journey is great. It is said that a handful of dirt from one's homeland is more precious than a thousand ounces of foreign gold."

伭奘三藏像

Hsuan-tsang and his imperial horse
begin their journey to the west.

It was now late autumn, and Hsuan-tsang with his attendants had journeyed to the interior, arriving at the first of an endless chain of mountains that would have to be crossed on the journey to India. As they began their ascent they lost the path they had been following and were beginning to search for a way back when all at once the ground gave way under their feet and they were plunged into a deep pit.

Hardly had they recovered their senses when they heard voices calling, "Seize them! Seize them!" When the travelers looked up, they saw fifty or sixty ogres crowding around the margin of the pit and peering down at them. Soon they were hauled out of the hole and brought before their captors' demon king. Tripitaka stared in disbelief at the leering monster, whose sawlike teeth were surrounded by steely whiskers. His claws resembled sharp swords.

The demon king was just ordering that the captives be bound and prepared for eating, when a great clamor was heard outside the camp and it was announced that the Bear Mountain Lord and the Steer Hermit had arrived. Tripitaka watched as the hideous ogres exchanged compliments and swaggered about. When the demon king asked how his guests had been getting on, one said, "Just doing as little as possible," while the other answered, "Only getting by."

At that moment one of Tripitaka's attendants began to groan from the tightness of his bonds, and one of the ogres asked, "How did these three get here?" Laughing, the demon replied, "They simply appeared at our door."

"May we impose on your hospitality?" the visitors asked.

"Of course. There is more than enough to go around.

Why don't we eat two of them, and save the third?" As all present roundly agreed, he gave the order for Tripitaka's attendants to be carved up at once. The heads, hearts, and livers were presented to the guests, the limbs to the hosts, and the remaining flesh and bones were distributed among the ogres. The munching and crunching of bones reminded Tripitaka of the sound a tiger makes when devouring a lamb. The scene was so hideous and frightening that Tripitaka's soul nearly left his body.

The ogres were still chewing bones and sucking marrow when the sun set, and it was dark before they began to retire. Tripitaka fell asleep in the depths of despair, having given up all hope of escaping with his life. Suddenly an old man appeared beside the reposed figure of Tripitaka, holding a staff in his hands. He waved his hand across Tripitaka's body and the binding ropes fell away. Then he blew into his face to rouse Tripitaka. The minute he came to his senses, Tripitaka fell to his knees, saying, "Thank you, venerable ancient, for saving my life."

The old man returned Tripitaka's bow. "Get up," he said, "have you lost anything?"

"My attendants have been eaten by the ogres. I have no idea what became of my horse and luggage."

"Isn't that your horse over there, with the saddle packs?" Tripitaka was astonished to see his horse, who he was sure had been either badly hurt or killed during the fall into the pit. Tripitaka looked from the horse to the old man. "Where am I?" he asked, rubbing his eyes, "and why is this place haunted by three ogres?"

"It is called Double Fork Ridge, and it is well known to be a place infested with tigers and wolves. The ogres you saw are various animal spirits and demons of mountains and trees. Yet because of the purity of your inner being, they could not devour you. Follow me, and I will lead you out of here and put you again on the right path."

Tripitaka adjusted the saddle packs and led his horse after the old man. When they were safely away, Tripitaka tied his horse to a tree and turned to thank the old man. Just then a gentle breeze began to stir, and instantly the old man was borne up into the air on the back of a crimson-crested white crane. When the wind subsided, a piece of paper came floating down and fell into Tripitaka's hand. It contained the following message:

> The Planet Venus from the Western Heaven
> Came to rescue you by Holy Command.
> In the course of your journey
> You will be assisted by divine disciples.
> Do not blame the scriptures
> For the hardships that lay ahead.

When Tripitaka finished reading the message he bowed toward the Heavens, saying, "My thanks to Gold Star for placing me once more on the true path."

12

Tripitaka Takes a Disciple

O̶N the following day Tripitaka came to a rugged mountain that seemed more attached to the sky than to the earth. It was only because of its indescribable beauty that he did not lose heart but began the steep and difficult ascent. He hadn't gone very far when he was startled by the appearance of a hunter perched on a large boulder. The hunter was shielding his eyes from the sun and looking out over the distant plain. They saluted each other. Tripitaka was about to climb up onto the boulder when he and the hunter were startled by a rumbling, guttural sound that took on the form of a human voice. "My Master has come, my Master has come," it said.

"What can that be, and what do the words mean?" Tripitaka said, as much to himself as to the hunter, who seemed not at all surprised.

"It must be that old monkey who's been locked up in an iron box at the base of the mountain."

"What old monkey?" Tripitaka asked, as startled by the explanation as he had been by the strange-sounding voice.

"This mountain was once called the Mountain of Five Elements. But after the Western campaign of our great T'ang Dynasty, it was renamed the Mountain of Two Frontiers. A few years ago I learned from an elder that when Wang-mang usurped the throne of the first Han Dynasty, this mountain was thrown down from Heaven in order to imprison a divine monkey. This monkey isn't affected by heat or cold, and he neither eats nor drinks. He is guarded by some local spirits who feed him iron pills when he is hungry, and give him the juice of molten copper when he is thirsty. One way or another, he is somehow kept alive. That was surely he who was crying out just now. You needn't be troubled. Why don't we go down and have a look?"

When they got to the base of the mountain, they came to an iron box that did indeed hold a monkey. He had managed to get his head out of the cage and with one free hand was waving wildly at Tripitaka and the hunter. "Master, where have you been? Welcome! Welcome! Get me out of here and I will see that you have a safe journey to India."

Tripitaka was afraid to move any closer, but the hunter approached the iron box and removed the grass from Monkey's hair and brushed the moss from his chin. "What do you have to say for yourself?" he asked.

"Nothing to you," Monkey said. "Tell that priest to come over here. I have a question to ask him."

"What is your question?" asked Tripitaka.

"Were you sent by the Emperor of T'ang to collect scriptures from India?"

"Yes," Tripitaka replied, "but what is that to you?"

Monkey replied, "I am the Great Sage, Equal of Heaven. Five hundred years ago I made a great ruckus in the Halls of Heaven. To atone for my sins the Buddha sealed me in this mountain. Not long ago the Bodhisattva Kuan-yin, who was commanded by the Buddha to find a pilgrim to bring some scriptures from India, came by this mountain and promised me that if I would straighten myself out and protect the pilgrim, I could be released from this stronghold and through my merits achieve salvation. I have been waiting night and day for you to arrive and set me free. I will follow you as a disciple and see that you are successful in obtaining the scriptures."

Tripitaka was delighted, but uncertain how to proceed. "Despite your good intentions," he said to Monkey, "I have neither an ax nor a chisel with which to set you free."

"No need," Monkey said. "You have only to wish me out, and out I will be."

"But how can that be?" Tripitaka asked.

"At the very top of this mountain," said Monkey, "there is a seal in golden letters, stamped by the Buddha himself. If you will go there and remove it, I will be free."

When Tripitaka turned to go up the mountain, the hunter took him aside and whispered, "How can you be sure that he is speaking the truth?"

"It's true! It's true!" Monkey screamed from his iron box. "Would I lie about a thing like this?"

After discussing the matter between them, Tripitaka and the hunter decided as a first step to go up the mountain to see if in fact the emblematic seal of the Buddha was really there. When they began to near the top of the mountain they saw ten thousand shafts of golden light and streams of hallowed air rising from a square slab of stone, whereon a seal in golden letters read OM MANI PADME HUM.

Tripitaka faced the West and knelt before the stone, saying in a tone of prayer, "If Monkey is ordained to be my disciple and to assist me in my quest of the scriptures, let these golden letters rise up, that he may be released and set free to serve my mission. But if he is not so ordained, and is only a cruel and deceitful monster, let this seal remain imprinted on this stone."

The words had barely escaped Tripitaka's mouth when a gust of wind blew up and carried the seal skyward, as an unearthly voice sounded: "I am the jailer of the Great Sage. Today his penance ends and this seal will return to the Buddha."

Overcome with piety, Tripitaka and the hunter bowed in the direction of the vanished seal and hurried down the mountain.

"The inscription is removed, Great Sage. You may now come out," Tripitaka announced.

"You'd better stand back," Monkey said. "I don't want to frighten you."

Tripitaka and the hunter withdrew, but Monkey exclaimed, "Farther, farther." They retreated for several leagues, but Monkey only shouted, "Farther still, farther still."

Suddenly they heard a thunderous crashing and grinding noise, and in the next instant Monkey was kneeling before Tripitaka, crying, "Master, I'm out!" Before Tripitaka could utter a word, Monkey jumped up and, brushing himself off, gathered up Tripitaka's packs and secured them to the horse's saddle. The horse trembled obediently before Monkey, in awareness of his divine origins, and Monkey, having once served as *pi-ma-wen* in the Jade Emperor's stables, was at his ease with an earthly horse.

When Tripitaka saw that Monkey knew how to make himself useful and was a person of good intentions, he said to him, "Disciple, we must give you a religious name."

"No need for that," Monkey said, "I already have a name. I'm called Aware-of-Vacuity."

As Monkey was speaking the hunter began adjusting his backpack, indicating that he was getting ready to depart. "Now that you two have found one another," he said, "you won't be needing me any longer."

"Thank you for your help," Tripitaka said. "Yes," Monkey concurred, "thank you for assisting my Master."

They watched the hunter go off by himself toward the plain, before they began their ascent of the mountain.

They had not gone far when they were stopped dead in their tracks by a savage tiger. The beast was growling and swishing its tail. Tripitaka reined in his horse, too terrified to speak. But Monkey seemed delighted. "Nothing to worry about, Master," he called out. "This tiger has come along at just the right moment, for I am in need of a new outfit." Taking the needle from behind his ear, Monkey made a magic pass and turned it into an iron cudgel. "I've been without my weapon for five hundred years, but today it is going to supply me with some needed clothing."

The tiger crouched down on the path, afraid to move. Monkey bellowed, "Cursed beast! Your time is up!" He raised his cudgel and brought it down square on the tiger's head. The blood gushed up like a spray of pomegranate blossoms, and the tiger's teeth flew out into space like tiny meteors of white jade.

Tripitaka was so terrified that he fainted and fell from his horse.

Turning his needle first into a knife and then into a darning needle, Monkey made himself a tiger-skin skirt. By the time Tripitaka came to, Monkey was ready to set out again, but this time in a far more ebullient mood.

"What became of the iron cudgel you slayed the tiger with?" Tripitaka asked. Puffing himself up, Monkey explained in great detail how he came to acquire his magic iron from the Dragon King's Palace, giving a full history of its origins and the various uses he had put it to since that time. Tripitaka then asked, "Why did that tiger, when it saw you approaching, lie down defenselessly and let you slay him?"

"That was nothing," Monkey said. "The fact is, even

dragons are terrified of me. In addition to monster slaying, I can make rivers turn back in their course and the seas boil up and overflow. I can look a person in the eye and discern his character. I can expand my body to fill the universe or reduce myself to a single strand of a down feather. In other words, there is no limit to my transformative powers. The slaying of that tiger was a mere hint of what I can do in a pinch. When we come to real difficulties, then you will see old Monkey shine."

Tripitaka was greatly relieved, and relaxing in his saddle, he urged his horse forward. Master and disciple chatted together and journeyed toward the sun as it slowly sank in the West.

The following morning, as the travelers were crossing a log at the edge of a swamp, they were met by six bandits heavily armed with spears, swords, knives, and bows. "Halt, priest!" they cried. "We want your horse and your packs. Be quick about it and we will spare your lives." Tripitaka was so frightened he fell from his horse. Monkey picked him up and said, "Don't be alarmed, Master, all this means to us is more clothes and money."

"Are you mad?" Tripitaka cried. "Are you deaf? Didn't you hear what they said? They said they are robbing *us*, but you are making it sound like we are about to rob *them*."

"Something like that," Monkey said. "Hold onto the horse and watch our belongings, and I will take care of these ruffians." Monkey strode forward with his arms folded and bowed to the bandits. "Why are you blocking the path of a humble priest?"

"We are the robber barons of the highways," they said,

悟空與賊
戰於廣野

Monkey and his iron cudgel deal with
a few bandits on the road.

"the nasty lords of the mountains. Our name is legion in these parts. Don't try to provoke our pity by your ignorance. Hand over your belongings at once and we will let you pass. If you so much as begin to pronounce the word 'No,' we'll make mincemeat of your flesh and powder of your bones."

"I am also a hereditary king," said Monkey, "and I have been a lord of the mountains for hundreds of years, so how is it that I've never heard of you?"

"If you really don't know who we are, we will tell you. We are called Eye that Sees and Delights, Ear that Hears and Grows Furious, Nose that Smells and Covets, Tongue that Tastes and Desires, Mind that Conceives and Lusts, and Body that Supports and Suffers."

Monkey laughed. "You're nothing but six hairy brigands! Don't you understand that we are priests and your masters? And yet you dare to block our way. Bring out your stolen treasures, and we will divide them into seven equal parts. My Master and I will take a seventh part and leave you the rest. In this way I will be willing to spare your lives."

The bandits stared at Monkey in amazement, uncertain whether to be angry or amused. Finally, one of them said, "You must be mad! You have just lost everything, and now you think you can barter with us using what is no longer yours." Brandishing their weapons, they fell on Monkey and began to send blows down on his head. After they had hacked away for ten minutes, they stopped, stood back, and looked Monkey up and down. "The priest has a hard head."

"Time for the Great Sage to perform," Monkey said, sliding the needle out from behind his ear. In the instant that the needle took to turn into an iron cudgel, the bandits turned on their heels to escape. But Monkey was too fast for them. Scattering blows left and right, he killed all six, stripped them of their clothing, and seized their belongings. Then he returned to Tripitaka and said, smiling, "Well, Master, we can continue on our way, I've exterminated the lot of them."

Tripitaka was flabbergasted. "You've done a terrible thing," he said. "However wicked those men might be, they never would have been sentenced to death in a court of law. You should have chased them away, not killed them. How can you think of yourself as a monk when you take another's life, and in this case not one, but six lives? You haven't a trace of mercy in you."

"Master, if I had not killed them, they would have killed you."

"I am a man of religion. I would rather die than kill another. And in this case, if I had been killed then only one would be dead, not six. How can you pretend to justify what you have done?"

"Listen here," Monkey said. "When I was a king five hundred years ago, I killed all kinds of people. How else could I have been king? How else become the Great Sage, Equal of Heaven?"

"It is precisely because you are undisciplined and lack scruples and self-control that you landed in the position of having to do penance for five hundred years. Now that you have become a priest you cannot go on behaving in the old way. If you do, then you are unworthy to be a priest and you will never return to the Western Heaven. Oh Monkey, you've been wicked! wicked!"

Monkey had never been able to take a scolding, and Tripitaka had just pushed him to the limit. "If that's how it is, if I'm not good enough to be a priest, if I'm not going to return to the Western Heaven, then I'm not going to India either. You can go yourself!" Shaking himself, Monkey somersaulted skyward, and in an instant he was out of sight.

"Well, well," Tripitaka said. "If that's how it is with that monkey I'm better off without him. I guess I wasn't meant to have a disciple. I'll just have to pull myself together and go on alone." Once again the priest arranged his bags, hoisted them on his horse, and with the staff in one hand and the reins in the other he walked on, disconsolate but determined to reach his destination.

13

The Cap of Discipline

*T*RIPITAKA had not gone far when he came upon an old woman carrying a silk brocaded robe and an embroidered cap. Tripitaka pulled aside to let her pass. "Where do you come from, venerable monk?" she asked, "and why are you traveling by yourself?"

"The Great King of China has sent me to the Western Heaven to fetch the true scriptures from the living Buddha."

"The Buddha of the West lives in the Temple of the Great Thunderclap. That's a journey of 108,000 miles. You'll never get there without a companion or disciple to assist you."

"I had a disciple," Tripitaka said. "I picked him up a few days ago, but he was a rough and unruly chap, and terribly headstrong. I had to be harsh with him in order to teach him a lesson, but he would have none of my scolding and disappeared without a trace."

"I have here a brocaded tunic and a cap with bands of inlaid gold that belonged to my son. He had entered a monastery and served as a monk for two or three days before he died. I have just returned from the monastery, where I mourned him at the temple. His master gave me these things to keep in his memory. Since you have a disciple, I will be glad to give you this tunic and cap."

"I am most grateful," Tripitaka said, "but as my disciple has departed I cannot accept your generous offer."

"Did you see which way he went?"

"All I heard was a whistling sound in the direction of the East."

"That's the direction I'm headed," the old woman said. "I'm bound to meet him on the way. I have a spell written out here that I would like to pass on to you, called True Words for Controlling the Mind, or the Headband Spell. You must learn it in secret, fix it in your memory, and never let it out. When I catch up with your disciple I'll give him a talking-to. After I've persuaded him to come back to you, give him this tunic and cap to wear. If he refuses to obey you, you have merely to recite the spell and he will do what he is told and will never again leave your side."

Tripitaka bowed his thanks, but in that same instant she had turned into a shaft of golden light and disappeared toward the East. Only then did he realize that the old woman was the Bodhisattva Kuan-yin in disguise. Tripitaka bowed again in the direction of the East, and taking a pinch of earth, he scattered it like incense after the Bodhisattva. He then packed up the tunic and cap and, sitting by the side of the road, began to recite the magic spell.

Riding his cloud trapeze, Monkey headed straight for the Palace of the Dragon King of the Eastern Ocean. After they had exchanged greetings, the Dragon King said, "I heard that your penance has been completed. Congratulations! I would have thought you'd be going back to your immortal mountain to be a king again among your little ones."

"I am indeed," Monkey said, "but no rush, no rush. You probably didn't know that I became a priest."

"How did that happen?"

"The Bodhisattva of the Southern Ocean persuaded me to seek the truth by becoming a disciple to a scripture pilgrim.

We were on our way to India to worship the Buddha and seek his commandments."

"In that case I congratulate you again. You have, as the saying goes, 'left the bad in order to attain the good.' But tell me, why are you traveling eastward, when your destination lies in the West?"

Monkey smiled self-consciously. "My Master doesn't understand human nature. We met some brigands on the road who wanted to rob us, so naturally I killed them. After that, this T'ang monk began nagging me, saying over and over again that I should have spared their lives and turned them over to a magistrate or some such rot. You know how I can't stand people criticizing me, and so I up and left. I thought I'd stop here for a spot of tea on my way home."

"All well and good," the Dragon King said, "all well and good. Thanks for coming. The tea will be here shortly. But shouldn't the Great Sage, Equal of Heaven, learn a little patience? If you don't learn to control your temper, take instruction, and submit to the will of another, you will end up an evil immortal after all. Is that what you want? Just think, this may be your last chance! No one can decide for you. You must ask yourself if it is wise to jeopardize your future by indulging in a little momentary comfort."

"Don't say another word," Monkey said. "Old Monkey will go back and fulfill his task and achieve what has been promised."

On his way back Monkey met the Bodhisattva Kuan-yin. "What are you doing here?" she scolded. "Why did you break your vow to me and abandon the scripture pilgrim?"

"Everything went as you said," Monkey replied, "but I didn't bargain on being scolded and nagged, so I gave him the slip and have just been to the Dragon King's Palace for tea. However, I've changed my mind, and I'm on my way back."

"Hurry up, then," the Bodhisattva said, "before you change your mind yet again. As it is, you will need to improve your performance."

"Don't worry about that," Monkey replied. "This time I've decided for myself."

Monkey returned to find Tripitaka sitting by the side of the road. "Why are you looking so dejected?" Monkey asked his master.

"Don't you know, you grievous monkey? I lost heart momentarily. But never mind that! Why did you leave so abruptly, and what has brought you back?"

"I just went to visit the Dragon King in the Eastern Ocean, to have some tea."

"Priests should not lie," Tripitaka said. "You've only been gone an hour, and you claim you've gone as far as the Eastern Ocean."

"That's not so hard as it sounds," Monkey replied. "With a single somersault on my cloud trapeze I can travel 108,000 miles."

"Just because I spoke to you a little sharply you picked yourself up and left in a huff. With your talents you can just dash off for a spot of tea, leaving me behind to hunger and thirst and struggle for myself."

"Master, if that's the case, I'll go beg some food for you."

"There's no need to beg," Tripitaka said, "there are some dried provisions in my bag."

When Monkey opened his Master's pack his eyes were dazzled by the sight of the tunic and cap. "Did you bring these with you from the East?" Monkey asked.

Thinking quickly, Tripitaka replied, "I used to wear them when I was young. By wearing the cap you can recite scriptures without having to learn them, and by putting on that coat you can perform ceremonies without having to practice them."

"Dear Master," Monkey implored, "how about letting me try them on?"

"Go ahead. If they fit you, you can wear them."

Tripitaka pretended to be eating, but under his breath he was reciting the spell. "Oh, my head," Monkey bellowed. "It's starting to hurt!" Tripitaka went on with the spell, and Monkey was soon rolling on the ground, writhing in pain. He began clutching at the cap in an attempt to tear it free.

Fearing that the cap would come loose, Tripitaka stopped reciting, and when he did, Monkey's pain instantly stopped. Monkey tried again to remove the cap, but it seemed to be rooted to his skull. Next he took the needle from behind his ear and tried to pry it loose. But it was no use.

Tripitaka began reciting once again, and this time the pain was so intense that Monkey's face turned red and his eyes began to bulge out of his head. At the sight of his agonizing pain Tripitaka took pity on him and stopped the spell, and again Monkey's pain disappeared.

"You put a spell on me," Monkey cried.

"Not at all," Tripitaka said, "I was just reciting the Headband Scripture. There's no spell in that."

Monkey said, "Recite it again and see what happens." Tripitaka began reciting and again the pain returned. "Stop! Stop!" Monkey pleaded. "Now I know it's the cause of the spell, so don't try to tell me you're not causing it."

"Now will you listen to my instructions?"

"I will," Monkey said, "and I won't cause any more trouble, or go flying off, or be unruly!"

"You'd better not," Tripitaka said, "or I will recite the spell."

"I wouldn't dare," Monkey said, "I wouldn't dare." But in his heart Monkey was not repentant. When Tripitaka turned away, he slipped out his needle and turned it into an iron cudgel. He was about to bring it down on his Master's head, when Tripitaka turned in time and began the magic recitation. Once again Monkey fell to the ground, writhing in pain. "I give up," he cried, "please, I give up."

"You wicked Monkey! Is it possible that you were about to strike me down?"

"No, no, no," Monkey chanted, "I wouldn't dare." Monkey was still groaning when he got to his feet. "Master," he said, "who taught you that spell?"

"An old woman gave it to me."

"That's all I needed to know," Monkey said. "You can't fool me, it was the Bodhisattva Kuan-yin. How dare she cause me such suffering? Just you wait, I'm off to the Southern Ocean to give her a thrashing!"

"Not so brash, you foolish monkey. If she taught me the spell, then she knows it herself, and a lot more besides. She'll make quick work of you if you dare confront her."

Once again Monkey was overwhelmed with contrition. He knelt before Tripitaka and said, "Master, this is all too much for me. I'll go with you to India, and you needn't be so quick to use the spell. I promise to follow you faithfully until we achieve our goal."

"In that case, help me mount my horse, and let's be on our way." Monkey tucked in his shirt and tightened his belt. He gathered the luggage together and put on his best smile as he fell in beside his master.

14

Riding the Dragon

TRAVELING now under the cold gray sky of winter, the priest and his disciple scaled peaks and passed under hanging cliffs as their way took them over dangerous mountain passes and slippery, ice-packed precipices. They came at last to Coiled Serpent Mountain. "I remember," Monkey said, "that there is a river in this chain of hills called Eagle Grief Stream."

They soon heard the distant sound of the torrent, and a moment later they arrived at the water's edge. Tripitaka had reined in his horse and was looking down at the churning river, when all at once a dragon came swirling out of the waves. Monkey hurriedly pulled Tripitaka from the horse and untied the baggage and threw it down on the bank. Grabbing Tripitaka by the arm, he hurried him up the ground. The dragon swooped down and swallowed the horse, halter and all, and then plunged back into the stream.

"What a bad dream, what a bad dream," Tripitaka murmured over and over. "How will I get to India without a horse? . . . It's too far to walk! . . . Oh, it's been eaten, been eaten. . . ." Mumbling to himself, Tripitaka began sobbing uncontrollably.

"Don't make such a spectacle of yourself," Monkey shouted, infuriated that Tripitaka was showing such signs of weakness and despair. "Just sit here without making a wretched scene, and I'll go convince that dragon to return our horse."

"Don't go," Tripitaka pleaded. "He's apt to come creeping back out, and this time he'll swallow me!"

"You're impossible, impossible!" Monkey roared. "You say you want your horse, but you won't let me go after it. I don't want to hear another word from you! Just sit here while I go take care of business."

Monkey hitched up his belt, straightened his tiger-skin skirt, and strode down to the river's edge. Using his magic powers, he created a turbulent storm in the stream. The dragon was trying to sleep off his lunch, but he soon saw that this was not going to be possible. He began talking to himself. "Blessings never repeat themselves, but troubles always come in pairs. It's barely a year since I was condemned to exile by the Heavenly Tribunal, and now this wretched monster is threatening to do me harm."

Seeing no way out, the dragon came exploding out of the waves and hissed at Monkey. "Where do you come from, strange monster, that you dare to challenge me?"

"Never mind my origins," Monkey said. "Just give me back my horse if you want to live."

"Too late," the dragon said. "Your horse is inside me now and is not about to come out. Besides, what can you do to me?"

"Take a look at this cudgel," Monkey said. "It's either my horse or your life." The dragon met the challenge, and a ferocious battle ensued on the banks of Eagle Grief Stream. With the fight tilting in Monkey's favor, the dragon turned himself into a tiny water snake and wriggled into the long grass.

Monkey parted the grass with his cudgel and began prancing wildly along the river's edge. He uttered the magic word OM as a summons to the local spirits and the god of the mountain, who appeared at once at his feet. "Expose your shanks," Monkey commanded, "so I can give you each five blows from my cudgel, just to relieve my suffering."

"Great Sage," they pleaded, "please allow us to defend ourselves. We had no idea that your penance had been served and that you had been released from captivity. Had we known, we would have been here to serve you. We humbly beg your forgiveness."

"All right, all right," Monkey said. "I'll desist from beating you this time, but tell me at once where this dragon came from and why he has swallowed my Master's white horse."

"This is all news to us," they said. "There didn't use to be any underwater monsters in these parts, until the Bodhisattva Kuan-yin rescued that dragon and put him here. The best plan now would be to have the Bodhisattva come out here and deal with it herself."

While the spirits were talking they heard from on high the voice of the Golden-Headed Guardian. "The Great Sage needn't be troubled, I will go and fetch the Bodhisattva."

"Go quickly," Monkey said, "and thanks for taking the trouble."

"No trouble at all," the Golden-Headed Guardian called back before soaring off on his cloud.

When the Golden-Headed Guardian reached the Bodhisattva and gave a full report, Kuan-yin said, "Why, that dragon is the son of Ao-jun, the Dragon King of the Western Ocean. Through carelessness he set fire to the palace and destroyed the magic pearls. His father accused him of subversion, and he was sentenced to death by the Heavenly Tribunal. I intervened and convinced the Jade Emperor to commute the dragon's sentence on condition that he serve to transport the scripture pilgrim to India. I don't understand how he could have gone and swallowed that monk's horse! I'll have to go down and have a look."

The Bodhisattva came down from her lotus platform, and

together they left the fairy cave and traveled on a luminous beam of light to Eagle Grief Stream.

When Monkey caught sight of Kuan-yin he began jumping up and down, screaming at the top of his lungs. "Some 'Teacher of the Seven Buddhas' you are! A fine 'Founder of the Faith of Mercy' you turned out to be! Why have you been plotting against me?"

Kuan-yin was just as furious. "You impudent stableman!" she shouted. "You addle-brained red-bottom! Have you forgotten what I went through to find a proper pilgrim, one who has been instructed to redeem you? Instead of thanking me, you just go on making more trouble!"

"You call that being saved? Instead of allowing me to run around and have some fun, I have to spend all my time looking after this impractical T'ang priest. And on top of that, you give him this magic cap that's now rooted to my head, and every time he says a magic spell I have these splitting headaches."

The Bodhisattva laughed. "Monkey, you are incorrigible. If I hadn't found a way to control you, Heaven knows what you might not have done by now! I'm trying to keep you on the straight and narrow—for your own good!"

"Don't try to shift the blame," Monkey said. "Just tell me why you went and put this dragon here after he had been condemned by the courts. Now he's eaten my Master's horse. His sins are all your fault, you know."

"It's true that I got the Jade Emperor to station the dragon here, but I did that because I needed him to carry the pilgrim to India. No ordinary Chinese horse would have been able to do that."

"Now you tell me," Monkey said. "Well, I've frightened him and he's afraid to come out. What are we to do now?"

Kuan-yin said to the Golden-Headed Guardian, "Go to

the edge of the stream and call out, 'Come out, third son of the Dragon King, come out! The Bodhisattva from the Southern Ocean is here and wants to see you.' He'll come out at once."

As soon as the dragon leapt out of the water and saw the Bodhisattva, he resumed his previous form. After saluting her and thanking her again for saving his life, he said, "I've had no news of the scripture-seeking pilgrim."

Pointing to Monkey, Kuan-yin said, "Haven't you met the scripture pilgrim's eldest disciple?"

Ao-jun recoiled. "He's my adversary. We've been at battle ever since I got hungry yesterday and ate his master's horse. He never said anything to me about scripture seeking. There hasn't been half a word between us."

"Monkey would much rather talk about his own powers than refer to the teaching," Kuan-yin said. "But in the future if either of you is questioned, you should say that you are seeking scriptures, and there won't be any more problems."

When they both agreed to follow her advice, Kuan-yin took her willow spray and sprinkled the dragon with the sweet dew in her vase. She then blew on him with her magic breath and cried, "Change!" The dragon changed instantly into the exact image of the Master's white horse. Then, in a soft but firm voice, she said, "You must work to atone for your sins and complete the task I have set for you. When this has been accomplished, you will have achieved your golden body of enlightenment." The horse thanked the Bodhisattva and promised to carry out his duties faithfully.

Placing the bit in the horse's mouth, Kuan-yin turned to Monkey and instructed him to lead the horse to Tripitaka. Monkey refused to budge, however, and said, "I'm not going, I'm not going. The journey to the West is long and treacherous. I'll never get there, dragging that ordinary monk along after me, not with the difficulties I've seen already, and there's no telling what lies ahead. I'm lucky to get out of this alive. What's the salvation in that?"

"How odd," the Bodhisattva said. "In the old days you were full of talk about enlightenment. I would think now, having escaped the punishment imposed on you by Heaven, you would be able to endure a hardship or two. Without faith and perseverance nothing is possible." Kuan-yin stopped and thought. "Perhaps you are in need of additional assistance. I hereby give you permission to call on both Heaven and Earth in times of trouble, and they will come to your assistance. And in the time of your greatest trials I myself will come to you. And now I shall endow you with one more power." Plucking three leaves from her willow spray and placing them on the back of Monkey's head, she cried, "Change!" and the leaves turned at once into three hairs with life-saving powers. "When you find yourself in a hopeless situation, use these according to your need."

Monkey thanked the Bodhisattva; taking the horse by the forelock, he led it to Tripitaka. "Master," he called out, "here's a horse for you, after all. And it's in much better shape than the last one!"

15

Pigsy and the Dragon of the River of Flowing Sands

*I*T was now early spring. The mountain forest had begun to robe itself in shades of new green. The plum blossoms had fallen, and the willow leaves had come into bud. The slow, gentle ascent of the winding path up the mountain was barely noticed by Tripitaka, but Monkey, ever watchful and in possession of extraordinary vision, carried in his mind a complete picture of the winding path that would lead over the mountaintop. He was able to see, far ahead, a sign above the entrance of a cave located on the side of a steep precipice that they would eventually have to pass.

Monkey was beginning to feel uneasy. Sensing that they might be entering a dangerous region, he decided to go ahead and see if the way was clear. "There's a sign above a cave that we'll be passing on our way over the mountain," Monkey said to Tripitaka. "I want you to stay here while I go and have a look."

"Can you read the sign over the cave?"

"Yes," Monkey said, "it says Cloud Ladder Cave. It could be the home of some demon or evil monster."

"What makes you say that?"

"Just a hunch, Master, just a hunch." But this time, when Monkey peered up at the cave again to have another look, he saw a pig-faced demon standing at the cliff's-edge entrance to the cave, holding a nine-pronged muckrake in his

猪悟能

Pigsy, with his nine-pronged muckrake,
tries to slip away from Monkey.

right hand. "Just as I thought!" Monkey exclaimed. Without another word of explanation, he somersaulted in the air and in a flash was standing on the very spot where the demon had stood just a second before.

But the monster was nowhere in sight. Monkey noticed that the cave door had been slammed tight. The crunching sound of the bolt lock could still be heard resounding through the cave. Monkey wasted no time. With one blow of his cudgel he smashed the door to bits. "Come out of there, you cowardly greaseball, and stand your ground against old Monkey!"

The monster was lying down inside, still huffing and puffing from his narrow escape from the ledge. He could still see before his mind's eye the flashing tiger skin that had come spinning up at him from out of the forest floor. But now he was angry. "No one can call me a greaseball and get away with it," he said under his breath, and he grabbed his muckrake as he made for the door.

"So it's you!" he said, on spotting Monkey. "The insufferable stableman! What have I done to you to cause you to come up here and break down my door? You had better go and have a look at the statute book: breaking and entering without a permit is a capital offense."

"You fool!" Monkey bellowed. "Don't waste your time reciting man-made laws to an immortal."

"So much for idle talk then," the monster said. "Open your mouth and receive a bite of my muckrake."

Monkey dodged the blow and, taunting the monster, said, "Isn't that something you use around the farm to dig up turnips and such? Don't try to fool me with your tools of the trade, you long-eared, short-legged, snout-faced lout!"

"You've made another mistake," the monster said. "This muckrake was given to me by the Jade Emperor."

"You'll have to think up a better lie than that," Monkey said. "Here's my head, go ahead and strike me, and we will see what kind of soul melting and spirit leaking you and your rake are capable of doing."

The monster came down on Monkey's head with such a cracking blow that sparks flew, but Monkey didn't even flinch. The monster let his arms fall to his side and looked at Monkey with astonishment. "What a head!" he exclaimed.

"Do you still think you know who I am?" Monkey taunted. "Or must I give you a complete rundown of my illustrious career?"

"I remember you well, you stinking red-bottom. You lived in your Water Curtain Cave surrounded by other bald-pates like yourself. That's the last I knew of your 'illustrious career.' So why are you here bothering me, crashing through my door and threatening my existence? I suppose you're carrying a permit for my arrest under some trumped-up charge."

"Not at all. Old Monkey is now a priest. I'm traveling to India with a scripture-seeking pilgrim called Tripitaka, who has been commissioned by the Emperor. I'm just clearing the way."

The monster's jaw dropped. "Where is the scripture pilgrim?" he gasped. "Please take me to him at once."

"Why do you want to see him?"

"I'm a convert of the Bodhisattva Kuan-yin. My religious name is Pigsy. She left me here, on a vegetarian diet, and said I was to wait for the pilgrim and assist him on his journey. In this way I would atone for my sins and achieve a just reward. I have been waiting for some years now without receiving any further instruction. If you are truly a disciple of the pilgrim, why didn't you say you were seeking scriptures instead of knocking down my door and making trouble with me?"

"How do I know you are not attempting to deceive me?"

Monkey said. "If what you say is true, turn and face Heaven and swear that you are telling the truth. Only then will I take you to see my Master."

Pigsy fell to his knees and kowtowed to the Heavens. "Dear Buddha," he cried out, "if I am not telling the truth, may I be cut into ten thousand pieces before the Heavenly Tribunal."

Monkey was pleased. "Good oath," he said. "Get up and I'll take you to my Master. But first you will have to burn down your lair." Pigsy hurriedly grabbed up some reeds and brambles and made a fire. The cave was soon reduced to a smoking kiln. "I have no other attachments," he said. "Now you can take me to the pilgrim."

"Hand over your rake," Monkey ordered. With the rake in his hand, Monkey plucked a hair from his side, blew on it with his magic breath, and cried, "Change!" It became a three-ply hemp rope, with which he bound Pigsy's hands. Then Monkey seized him by the ear and marched him out of the cave and down the mountain, shouting, "Hurry up! hurry up!"

"Can't you be a little gentle?" Pigsy pleaded. "You're hurting me."

"Can't do it," Monkey said. "As the proverb goes, 'The better the pig, the harder to hold.' After the Master has seen you and is convinced that you are in earnest, then I will let you go free."

When Pigsy saw Tripitaka, he fell on his knees. "Master, forgive me for not knowing you were here." While he was kowtowing, Monkey turned the binding cord back into a muckrake. Banging Pigsy on the head, he said, "Speak up, fool, tell the monk what he needs to hear."

Pigsy gave a full account of how the Bodhisattva had converted him. Tripitaka was very pleased. Burning some incense, he bowed toward the South, saying, "Thanks to the Bodhisattva for her holy grace."

Pigsy kowtowed again to Tripitaka, making a solemn vow to follow him to the West, and then he turned and bowed to Monkey as the senior disciple, calling him "Elder Brother."

The fair earth that had been warmed by the fires of the pomegranate blossoms turned cool as new lilies appeared on the ponds. Cicadas sang in the willow tree, and the fire star rolled toward the West. Summer had given way to fall.

The three travelers came to a huge and turbulent river of rolling waves. "My disciples," Tripitaka said, "this is a very broad river, and there isn't a boat in sight. How are we going to get across?"

"Those are terrible waves," Pigsy said. "A boat couldn't do much in water as rough as that."

Monkey sprang up into the air and, shading his eyes with one hand, gazed across the river. "This is big trouble, Master. Not for me, of course. With one shake of my hips I would be across. But for you—impossible!"

Standing up in his saddle, Tripitaka gazed over the top of the incoming waves. "I can't see across. How far is it?"

"About eight hundred miles," Monkey said.

Pigsy asked, "How do you figure it, Brother? That was a pretty quick calculation."

"I'll be frank with you," Monkey said. "These eyes of mine are so trustworthy that I can see up to a thousand miles away in daylight. I couldn't tell you the length of this river, but its width is a good eight hundred miles."

Tripitaka let out a deep sigh and pulled back his horse. Then, to his surprise, he spotted a stone slab with the inscription *River of Flowing Sands*. Beneath the name a short verse was inscribed:

> On these Floating Sands, eight hundred wide
> Weak waters flow, three thousand deep.
> On its surface not a goose feather floats
> While rush petals quickly sink to the deep.

As they were reading this, the waves rose in a mountainous spray to reveal a hideous monster covered in flaming red hair, with lanterns for eyes, wearing a flowing yellow cape and carrying a priest's staff, with a string of nine skulls hanging from his neck.

The monster came rushing straight in their direction. Monkey grabbed Tripitaka and made a dash for high ground. Pigsy swung his muckrake around and aimed a blow at the monster's head. Using his priestly staff, the monster fended off the blow. It was a good fight, evenly matched, with first Pigsy taking the advantage, and then the nine-skulled monster; it went twenty rounds without a victor being declared.

Meanwhile, Monkey was holding onto the reins of the horse, guarding the luggage and keeping a careful eye on Tripitaka. But as the fight waged on he began to grind his teeth and clench his fists. Itching to get into the fray, and unable to control himself any longer, he whipped out his rod. "Master," he said, "sit here and don't be afraid, Monkey needs to get in a few licks." Tripitaka began to protest, but Monkey gave a loud whoop and went flying toward the scene of action.

Pigsy and the monster were tightly locked in combat, leaving no opening for Monkey. Darting this way and that, however, he was able at last to bring down a crushing blow on the monster's head with his iron cudgel. The monster was badly shaken, but he was able to make his way to the water's edge and quickly plunged into the waves.

Pigsy was furious. "Hey, Brother," he said, "who asked you to butt in? He was just beginning to tire; another four or five rounds and I would have captured him. But one look at your ugly face and he beat a hasty retreat. You spoiled it!"

"I couldn't control myself," Monkey said. "It's been too long since I've had a really good fight. How was I to know that the monster wouldn't enjoy a good tussle?" By the time Monkey had finished making his apologies they were both laughing and joking; they flung their arms over each other's shoulders as they walked back toward Tripitaka.

"Well, did you catch the monster?" Tripitaka asked.

"We were too much for him," Monkey said. "He gave up the fight and jumped back into the river."

"Too bad," Tripitaka said. "I was sitting here thinking that the monster might be able to get us across this river. After all, who would better know where the shallows and the currents are?"

"Precisely," Monkey shouted. "As the proverb goes, 'The one near cinnabar turns red, the one near ink becomes black.'"

Pigsy said, "If we catch him, we won't kill him but merely constrain him to carry the Master over on his back." Turning to Monkey, he continued, "This time the chance is yours. I'll stay with the Master, and you go off and tame the dragon."

"I'm not at home in the water," Monkey said. "To get around at all down there I have to make a magic sign and recite a water-repelling spell. Either that or turn myself into a crab, shrimp, or fish, or some other such creature. Up in the clouds, or atop mountains, that's when I can do my stuff, but down there, in the constraining deeps, I'm not good for much."

Pigsy said, "In former times, when I was Marshal of the

Heavenly Rivers, I had a force of eighty thousand sailors under my command, and I knew more than a little about that element. What worries me is that he may have some clansmen with him down there, and in that case I wouldn't stand a chance."

"The thing to do," Monkey said, "is to lure him out here before he gets the advantage. Once he's out of the water, old Monkey will join in the fight."

"Right you are," Pigsy replied. "That plan is bound to succeed." Stripping off his blue tunic and removing his shoes, he held his rake with both hands and dove into the water.

The monster, who was napping just then, was startled awake by the gushing sound of waves being made by Pigsy's rake. "Look where you're going, you ham hock," he hollered, "or I'll drive my staff down your throat." Pigsy fended off the blow with his rake, crying, "What sort of monster are you, that you dare to block my path?"

"You mean to say you don't recognize me? I'm not some fiend or demon, as you think, but a divinity with a proper name and surname."

"If that's true," Pigsy said, "what are you doing down there in the watery deep, preying on human lives? Come clean with Pigsy and pronounce your name, or I'm bound to run you through."

"I was an alchemist, skilled in the arts, who was summoned to Heaven by the Jade Emperor and promoted to Curtain-Raising Captain. One fateful day, while serving guests at the Jasper Pool during the Festival of Immortal Peaches, I dropped and broke a crystal cup of jade. The Emperor was furious and ordered my execution, but the Red-Legged Immortal had my sentence changed and I was banished to the River of Flowing Sands. Now I must get by as best I can. When I'm hungry I go ashore and prey on woodcutters and fishermen. As it turns out, you've called at a very good time. Though you are coarse and ugly, when I've had you chopped up well and served with a fancy sauce, I think you'll do just fine."

Pigsy was furious. "Coarse, indeed! Don't think you can talk to me like that and get away with it. I'm not a seasoned meat loaf to satisfy a loathsome appetite, or a piece of bacon to be thrown on the fire and forgotten. If you want to taste something, take a lick of this muckrake."

Once again a great battle ensued between Pigsy and the monster of the deep. The waves churned like exploding lava, causing tidal waves that rocked the hills and flooded the tributary streams. The two adversaries were matched in their fury, like a brass pan meeting a metal broom, a jade gong confronting a golden bell.

Feigning defeat, Pigsy suddenly withdrew to the surface and, dragging his rake behind, ran across the waves toward shore. "Come up onto dry land, and I'll square the match," he hollered over his shoulder.

Monkey had been watching the contest with baited breath. Unable to control himself, he charged into battle just when Pigsy and the monster reached shore. Seeing Monkey with his cudgel raised on high, the monster turned and dove back in the water.

"You impatient ape!" Pigsy screamed. "You've ruined it again! If you had let me lead him to high ground, you could have blocked his path to the river. We would have caught him for sure. Now he's back in his element and we'll never be able to coax him out again."

"Don't shout at me, you idiot. Let's go see the Master."

When they reached high ground and found Tripitaka, they explained their predicament. "Now what will we do?" Tripitaka said, convinced that they had lost their last chance.

"Relax, Master," Monkey said, "I have a good idea. I'm going to leave at once for the Southern Ocean."

"What will you do there?" Pigsy asked.

"This scripture-seeking business was an invention of the Bodhisattva's," Monkey said. "She was the one who converted us. Let's see if she has some better way of getting us across this river than fighting with that slimy water-loving monster."

"Elder Brother," Pigsy said, "when you get back there put in a good word for me."

"If you are going," Tripitaka said, "you'd better leave at once."

"Not to worry," Monkey said, "I'll be back before you know I'm gone."

"I've heard all about your cloud-somersaulting skills," Pigsy said. "If it's so easy for you, why can't you lift the Master and do a double flip across this river? That would put an end to our monster-taming enterprise."

"Listen here, Pigsy, you also know how to ride the clouds. If it's so easy, why don't you take the Master across?"

"Mortal flesh and bone are as heavy as Mount T'ai. Simple cloud-soaring magic isn't good enough; but I thought your famous cloud-somersaulting would be able to turn the trick."

"I can go farther than you, and faster, but our two kinds of soaring are essentially the same. If you can't carry him, what makes you think I can? An old proverb says, 'Lift Mount T'ai, it's as light as a mustard seed, but don't try to raise a mortal above the earthly dust.' I have more spells than that monster in the deep, but when he assaulted Tripitaka, I had to drag the Master along the ground. To escape the sea of sorrows our Master must make his way through all these strange territories. We are the mere guardians of his mortal life, but we can't protect him from his travails, nor can we go ahead and obtain the scriptures by ourselves. Each to his own level and according to his being. Even if we went ahead and saw the Buddha by ourselves, he could not give us the scriptures. Remember the adage: 'What's easily gotten is soon forgotten.' "

Monkey turned and somersaulted off onto his cloud and in less than a half hour he came in sight of the Southern Ocean and saw Mount Potalaka rise up before him. He dropped down from his cloud at the edge of the Purple Bamboo Grove, where he was met by the Spirits of the Twenty-Four Ways. "Great Sage, what brings you here?" they asked.

"My Master is in trouble, and I have come to seek advice from the Bodhisattva."

"Please be seated," the spirits said, "and we will announce you." When Monkey was shown in, the Bodhisattva was leaning on the balcony overlooking the flowers in the Lotus Pool, with the Pearl-Bearing Dragon Princess at her side. After Monkey had prostrated himself before her, she asked, "Why aren't you accompanying your Master? For what reason are you here?"

"After crossing Yellow Wind Ridge we came to the River of Flowing Sands, a body of weak water eight hundred miles across. This river is guarded by a monster and we cannot get across. I myself and Pigsy, a disciple we picked up on the way, engaged him in battle, thinking we could subdue him, but we have not been successful. That's why I am here, to ask that you in your mercy help us find some way out of our dilemma."

"Here it is, all over again," Kuan-yin scolded. "Why didn't you tell the monster that you were accompanying your Master, a scripture-seeking pilgrim, to India?"

"We were too busy trying to capture him to get into any lengthy discussions."

"Don't you understand? I put that monster there on purpose to help the T'ang monk. If only you had mentioned that you had come from China to seek scriptures, that monster would have revealed his true identity and come into your service."

"At the moment," Monkey said, "he's skulking at the bottom of the river. I don't see how we can possibly enlist him now."

The Bodhisattva summoned her disciple, Hui-an. Taking a red gourd from her sleeve, she handed it to him, saying, "Take this gourd and travel with Monkey to the River of Flowing Sands. There you must shout, "Sandy!" He is sure to come out, and when he does, take him to the Master so that he may submit and become a disciple. Next, take the nine skulls he wears around his neck and arrange them according to the position of the Nine Palaces. Finally, put the gourd in the center and you will have a dharma vessel capable of ferrying Tripitaka across the river."

After reporting to Tripitaka, Hui-an walked down to the river's edge and called out to Sandy, as he had been instructed to do. When Sandy heard his religious name, he knew at once that he was being beckoned by the Bodhisattva. When he emerged from the waves he asked Hui-an, "Where is the pilgrim?" Hui-an pointed toward the river bank, but when Sandy spotted Pigsy, he said, "I fought with that lout for two days, and he never said a word about scriptures. And that ape sitting next to him is his partner in crime. You won't get me within a dragon's tail of those two characters."

"But those are the pilgrim's disciples. They too, like yourself, were converted by the Bodhisattva. You have nothing to fear from them."

*After putting up a fight, Sandy joins
the quest for scriptures.*

Sandy scrambled up the bank and bowed to Tripitaka. "Please forgive me for failing to recognize you. I don't know how I could have been so blind."

"You scoundrel," Pigsy said, "why did you put up a fight when you could have joined us in the quest for the scriptures?"

"Are you truly willing to dedicate yourself to our mission?" Tripitaka asked Sandy.

"I have already been converted by the Bodhisattva," Sandy said. "There is no question."

"Very well," Tripitaka said. Calling Monkey over, he commanded, "Go fetch the sacred razor and shave the disciple's head."

16

Flaming Mountain and
the Iron Fan

*T*HE seasons passed and with the seasons, the years. Each new adventure and difficulty provided an experience from which the travelers had something specific to learn. Their journey thus seemed to be without end, for each of the disciples and the Master in particular had much to learn. They needed to be tested in the iron-hard realities of life, until they had been made malleable and trustworthy servants of the Way.

Tripitaka had the dual task of mastery over himself and his disciples, and each disciple had his own weakness to overcome besides having to learn to respect the functions that the others performed. For it is no easy matter to see that each one is related to the Whole, and that the Whole is One.

The white horse had the responsibility of carrying the Master. Monkey was responsible for the Master's safety, and Pigsy was in charge of the luggage, while Sandy had to lead the horse and care for its needs. What all of them had in common was a wish, but standing between each one and that wish was his dual nature. This produced conflict between the heart—the place where the wish was buried—and the needs of the lower nature, which often forgot what the spirit yearned for.

Instead of facing the conflict in themselves, however, the companions often fought with one another. Monkey was impatient with the mortal limitations of Tripitaka; Pigsy was jealous of Monkey because he didn't seem to have a physical burden to bear; Sandy preferred to sit back and let others take the lead, while the white horse remained a mysterious, silent partner.

One day Pigsy said to Monkey. "Elder Brother, how much do you think this load weighs that I am carrying?"

"Brother," Monkey answered, "since you and Sandy joined us I haven't had that duty, so how should I know what it weighs?"

"Without going into any great detail," Pigsy said, "such as counting each of the items, let's just say it is a heavy load and that I deserve some pity. The Master treats you like a disciple, but he treats me like a hired hand."

"If you're complaining to me, you can save your breath. My job is to look after the Master's safety, Sandy's in charge of the horse, and you have the luggage to carry. You had better hold up your end, or you'll feel Monkey's cudgel on your shanks."

"Don't start bullying me," Pigsy cried. "I know you're too high and mighty to carry the luggage, but that huge horse of the Master's is strong enough to carry more than one old monk. Couldn't you suggest that he carry one or two pieces of luggage?"

"Watch who you're calling a horse," Monkey said. "He's no ordinary earthly horse, but the son of Ao-jun, the Dragon King of the Western Ocean. Because he set fire to the palace and destroyed some pearls he was condemned by Heaven, but Kuan-yin saved his life and placed him in the Eagle Grief Stream to await the coming of the scripture pilgrim. When that happened the Bodhisattva appeared to take off his scales and horns and turned him into a white horse. Like us, he too is achieving merit, so we mustn't impose on him."

Sandy was listening in on their conversation. "Is it true, Elder Brother? Is he really a dragon?"

"Yes," Monkey replied, "it is true."

144

"I have heard an old saying," Pigsy offered, "that dragons can breathe out clouds, kick up dirt and make the sand fly, leap over mountains and stir up rivers and the seas. All I see before me is an ordinary horse just walking along."

"If you want to see what a dragon-horse can do," Monkey said, "I'll show you." He shook his cudgel, and the horse was instantly showered in ten thousand shafts of golden lights. The horse was so afraid that Monkey would strike him with his cudgel that he took off like a bolt of lightning. Tripitaka was unable to control him, and he didn't stop until he reached the top of the peak, where he was halted by the sudden unexpected sight of a red glow on the distant horizon that rose up like a mountain of flames.

The Master and his disciples came to the summit of the peak and began staring at the billowing red clouds on the horizon. The sheen of the white horse, as the result of his long run, took on a soft rosy glow.

"We're in autumn," Tripitaka said, "yet it is so hot. Why does the heat feel so intense?"

"Don't you know," Pigsy said, "that there is a kingdom in the West where the sun sets? The people there call it Sky's Brink. Every evening their king sends his people to the city walls to bang the drums and blow bugles to drown out the sound of the boiling sea, for when the sun falls into the ocean there is a great hissing and sizzling sound of fire cooking water. If the drums and bugles didn't smother that sound, all the little children in the city would die. Judging by the stifling heat, I would say we have reached that place."

Monkey burst out laughing. "Don't talk nonsense, you idiot. We're a long way from Sky's Brink, and between the Master's dithering, your loitering, and Sandy's indecisiveness, we won't get there if we travel from childhood to old age three times over."

"All right, Brother," Pigsy said, "if this isn't the place where the sun sets, then explain to me why it's so hot."

"Maybe the climate's out of sorts," Sandy said. "It may simply be an autumn heat wave."

As they were arguing, Tripitaka noticed several buildings of red brick on the side of the road, all with red tile roofs, red painted doors and gates, and red lacquered benches. "Monkey," the Master ordered, "go to one of those buildings and find out why we are experiencing this frightful heat."

Monkey put away his cudgel, straightened his clothes, and went swaggering up the road like a country gentleman. As he entered the gate leading to one of the buildings, an old man emerged from the main door. He wore a hemp robe that was neither yellow nor red, his straw hat was not quite blue and yet not quite black, his knobby bamboo staff was neither crooked nor straight, and his leather boots weren't old, nor were they quite new. He had a copper-red face and a white beard like braided yarn. His blue eyes were shaded by a shaggy brow, and when he smiled his teeth shone like gold.

The old man was startled to see Monkey. "What kind of freak monster are you, and what are you doing at my gate?" he asked. Monkey bowed respectfully and said, "Don't be afraid. I am not a freak but a disciple of a T'ang monk who has been sent by imperial commission to seek scriptures in the West. I have come to your gate at my Master's instructions to ask about this heat we are experiencing, and to learn the name of this land."

The old man was relieved and, smiling, said, "Forgive me, monk, my eyes must have been playing tricks on me. I didn't realize you were a priest."

"You needn't apologize," Monkey said.

"Where is your Master?"

"That's him, over there," Monkey said, "the one on the white horse."

The old man was delighted. "Please tell him to advance. I would like to meet him." Monkey waved Tripitaka and the others over. They all came and bowed before the old man, who was very taken with Tripitaka's auspicious appearance. He was also somewhat taken aback by Pigsy and Sandy. Despite his misgivings over Tripitaka's disciples, however, he was obliged to invite them in for tea and a meal.

After the houseboys had waited on them and they were comfortably settled, Tripitaka asked the old man why they were experiencing such intense heat during the autumn season.

"This unworthy region goes by the name of Flaming Mountain," the old man answered. "It's hot here all year round. There is no such thing as seasons here."

"Where is the mountain?" Tripitaka asked. "Does it block the way to the West?"

"Yes, that is so, it blocks the way. You can't get to the West from here. The mountain sits squarely in your path. Although it is sixty miles away, it sits in the middle of the eight hundred miles of flame. Not a single blade of grass can grow in these parts. Even if you had a bronze skull and a body of iron you would melt trying to cross that mountain."

Tripitaka turned pale and fell silent. But Monkey jumped up and said, "How do you get flour for your bread?"

"For that we are dependent on Immortal Iron Fan."

"What can you tell us about this immortal?" Monkey asked.

"The immortal you ask of has a palm leaf fan. One swish of that fan will put out the fire, the second swish will produce a wind, and the third swish brings the rain. This is how we sow and reap and produce the five grains. Without that immortal fan nothing would grow in the region."

"Where does this Immortal Iron Fan live?" Monkey asked.

"Why do you ask?"

"If he will lend us his fan we will be able to extinguish the flames on that mountain, and the people will be able to plant their crops in season."

"Not a bad idea," the old man said. "But you can't entice the immortal without presents."

"What sort of presents?" asked Tripitaka.

"Every ten years we go to visit the immortal. We take four hogs and four sheep, rare flowers and the fruits of the season, chicken, geese, and our best wines. After purifying ourselves in ritual baths, we ascend the immortal's mountain and beseech him to exorcise his magic over the mountain on our behalf."

Monkey asked excitedly, "Where is this mountain located? What is it called? How far is it from here? I'll go at once and get the fan!"

"The mountain is southwest of here," the old man replied. "It is called Mount Emerald Cloud. On that mountain there is a cave by the name of Palm Leaf Cave. The journey there and back takes us a month, as the round trip distance comes to 1,460 miles."

"Distance doesn't matter," said Monkey with a smile. "I'll be there and back in no time at all."

"Wait!" the old man cried. "Have something to eat and drink first, and take along some provisions. You'll need at least two companions, as there are no human habitations on the mountain; only tigers and wolves dwell there. You can't just go dashing off like a madman."

"No need for any of that," Monkey replied, laughing. "I'm off!" Hardly were the words out of his mouth when he disappeared through the door and ascended on his cloud trapeze.

"My lord!" the old man called after Monkey. "He is a cloud-soaring divinity! Who ever would have thought it!"

17

Fanning the Fire

*T*HE first thing Monkey heard when he arrived at Mount Emerald Cloud was a woodcutter chopping in the forest. Monkey approached the woodcutter and said, "Greetings, brother!"

"Where are you headed?" the woodcutter asked, after bowing to Monkey.

"If this is Mount Emerald Cloud," Monkey said, "perhaps you can help me. I'm looking for the Palm Leaf Cave belonging to the Immortal Iron Fan."

The woodcutter smiled. "The Palm Leaf Cave is here all right, but there is no Immortal Iron Fan, only a Princess Iron Fan, also known as Rakshasi."

"I've heard that this immortal has a palm leaf fan that can extinguish the Flaming Mountain. Would that be the demon Rakshasi?"

"Yes, she's the one. She protects the people who live beyond here for a price, and they have given her the name Immortal Iron Fan, but we have no need of her exorcizing powers, so we know her only as Rakshasi, the wife of the mighty Bull Demon King."

The color drained from Monkey's face. "Not one demon," he thought, "but two. This isn't going to be as easy as I thought."

The woodcutter noticed that Monkey had fallen silent. "Don't be troubled," he said. "Since you are on the Way, I'm sure you'll have no trouble finding the Palm Leaf Cave. Just follow this path eastward for about five miles, and you will come to it."

ॐ

The cave entrance was covered with lichen and moss. Wild cranes had built their nests in the bordering pines, while orioles spoke from the sad willow trees. Monkey looked down at the bordering stream, thinking it to be a place where old dragons would hide.

As Monkey stood before the entrance contemplating his next move, a young maiden stepped out, holding a flower basket in one hand, with a hoe over her shoulder. Although she was dressed in rags, Monkey could see that her heart was set on the Way. He went up to her with his palms pressed together and said, "Would you please announce me to your princess? I'm actually a monk on my way to the West to acquire some scriptures. I have come to borrow her palm leaf fan so that my companions and I can cross the Flaming Mountain."

"Please give me your name," the young girl said, "so that I may announce you. Also the name of your monastery."

"I am the Handsome Monkey King, but my name in religion is Aware-of-Vacuity. We are traveling from the East."

The young girl went back inside the cave and knelt before Rakshasi. "There is a monkey king outside the cave. He wishes to borrow your palm leaf fan so that he can cross the Flaming Mountain. He comes from the Land of the East."

Rakshasi's face turned red with rage. "That insolent ape, that devilish slayer of monsters and demons! He's undoubtedly come here to upset my schemes and steal my power. Doesn't he think I know who he is?" She commanded her assistants to bring out her weapons, and sporting two treasure swords of blue steel, she marched out of the cave, shouting, "Where's the monkey? Where's the monkey?"

"Greetings, Your Highness," Monkey said, stepping out from the shadow of a tree, as he pressed his palms together and bowed.

"Who asked for your greetings?" she said. "Back away and let me have a good look at you. You're not at all formidable. But I don't doubt that you've earned your reputation, somehow or other."

"Now listen here," Monkey began.

"Don't 'Listen here' me," she shot back. "Stop flapping your tongue and stretch out your head while I take a few whacks with my sword. If you can stand the pain, the fan is yours. If not, you can send me a message from Hell, where you can take up the matter of my fan with your King Yama."

"Enough said, Sister," Monkey replied and, folding his arms, he walked forward. "Here's my head. Hack at it all you like. But when you're finished with your carving, you must lend me your fan."

Rakshasi drew both her swords out at once and brought them down on Monkey's head. Blow upon blow rained down, but to no avail. When she realized that she had been tricked, she turned away and started to run.

"Where are you going, sister?" Monkey shouted after her. "Let me have your fan!"

"My fan! My treasure!" she gasped. "Never!"

"In that case you're going to have to taste my cudgel." Seizing her with one hand, Monkey reached behind his ear and quickly turned his needle into a rod. But Rakshasi struggled free and faced him with raised swords. They fought head to head, neither one giving way an inch. When she saw that she could not subdue Monkey on even terms, Rakshasi took out her fan, made a single swish, and blew Monkey out of sight. She replaced her swords and marched back into the cave in triumph.

Monkey blew across the sky like a fallen leaf in a whirlwind. He went twirling in the air through the long night, and it was morning before he came to rest atop a mountain peak. When he looked around he realized that he was on Little Sumeru Mountain. "What a terrible woman," Monkey said, letting out a deep sigh. "Terrible and powerful! How ever did she manage to send old Monkey back to this place?" As he looked around, wondering what he might do next, it suddenly occurred to him that the Bodhisattva Ling-chi had his residence on this mountain.

At that moment he heard the temple bells resounding in the distance. He scrambled down the slope and headed straight for the monastery, where he was recognized by the monk at the front gate. After he had been announced, Monkey was ushered in to see the bodhisattva.

"Allow me to congratulate you," Ling-chi said. "I assume you have acquired the sacred scriptures from the Buddha and are now returning to the East."

"Not yet," Monkey said. "I am sorry to say that we are not yet in sight of our goal."

"In that case, what brings you to our humble mountain?"

"We have been through countless ordeals," Monkey said, "and we have come at last to the Flaming Mountain, so we are nearing our destination. And yet, in another way, I feel we have never been farther away, for we are unable to proceed. The natives tell us that the only way we can extinguish the fire is with the magical palm leaf that is in the possession of the Immortal Iron Fan. It turns out that this immortal is the wife of the Bull Demon King, and she has no intention of letting me use her secret weapon. It was by the wind of that fan that I was blown all the way back to this mountain. For this reason I am calling on you now. Perhaps you can tell me the distance between here and the Flaming Mountain."

Ling-chi smiled. "That woman is called Rakshasi, or Princess Iron Fan. Her palm leaf fan is a miraculous spiritual treasure that was formed by Heaven and Earth after the Primordial Chaos. That leaf is the very essence of the negative yin principle. Not only can it put out fires, but if a man is fanned by it, he will be blown for eighty-four thousand miles before the negative wind subsides. There are fifty thousand miles between this place and the Flaming Mountain. It is only because of your cloud-somersaulting prowess that you were able to stop at all. No mortal would have been able to stop so soon."

"Terrible! Terrible!" Monkey exclaimed. "How will my Master ever overcome this hurdle and cross that burning mountain?"

"Don't worry, Great Sage," the bodhisattva said. "Your landing here is a sure sign that Tripitaka is fated to succeed."

"I don't understand."

"Long ago, when I was under the Buddha's tutelage, he presented me with a Wind-Arresting Pill and a Flying-Dragon Staff. The Flying-Dragon Staff has been tried, but the Wind-Arresting Pill has never been used. I will give it to you now, and her fan will no longer have any effect on you. You have but to acquire that fan and extinguish the fire, and your journey will be completed."

Monkey bowed and thanked the bodhisattva, who took from his sleeve a silk pouch containing the Wind-Arresting Pill. The pellet was sewn into Monkey's collar, where it was sure to be safe. "I won't detain you any longer," Ling-chi said. "Hurry toward the northwest, and you will soon come to the mountain home of Rakshasi."

Taking his leave, Monkey rode his somersault cloud back to the Jade Cloud Mountain. Banging on the cave entrance with his cudgel, he shouted, "Open up! Open up! Old Monkey's come to borrow your fan!"

The maid inside the door hurried back to report to her mistress. "Your Highness, that Monkey is back to borrow your fan."

This time Rakshasi was alarmed. "That wretched ape has a trick or two up his sleeve. He should have been blown eight-four thousand miles away. How did he get back so soon? This time I'll fan him two or three times, so that he'll never be able to find his way back to me." Putting on her armor and sheathing her swords, she marched out of the cave and challenged Monkey for the second time. "You stinking ape, aren't you afraid of me? Or have you returned in order to be killed?"

"Don't be so stingy, sister," Monkey said. "You simply have to lend me your fan, and I will leave you alone. I will give you my word as a gentleman that I will return it as soon as I am done with it. I am someone who is known for his honesty, not the kind of person who borrows something and then doesn't return it."

"You troublesome chimp! You are as impudent as you are baldpated. You've made trouble in Heaven, but you won't make trouble with me. If you try to stand your ground against me, we will see just how firmly your feet are planted to the earth." Rakshasi pulled the fan out from her sleeve and fanned Monkey. But at the same instant Monkey swallowed the Wind-Arresting Pill.

This time Monkey didn't move. "Fan all you like," he said. "If I move even an inch, I'm not an immortal."

Rakshasi fanned again and again, but nothing happened. Terrified, she stashed her fan away and ran back inside the cave. Monkey gave himself a shake and turned into a gnat.

Finding a crack in the door, he crawled inside the cave and was soon in the same room with Rakshasi. She was being brought a pot of tea, which she had ordered to help soothe her nerves. The maid nervously filled her cup. When Monkey saw that the surface of the cup was frothy, he jumped into her cup and hid inside the foam. At the first swallow Monkey went sliding down Rakshasi's stomach, where he changed himself into a miniature of his true form. "Sister!" he called up. "Lend me your fan!"

Rakshasi went pale. "Little ones," she cried out, "have you locked the front door?"

"Yes, Your Highness," they called back, "we certainly have."

"Then why do I hear Monkey bellowing in the chambers?"

"His voice is coming from inside your body," one of the maids said.

"Monkey!" Rakshasi screamed. "Why are you playing tricks on me?"

"These aren't tricks," Monkey said. "I don't play tricks. My magic and my powers are all real. Right now I am enjoying myself in your honorable belly. I feel now that I know you inside out, or, as the saying goes, 'I'm beginning to see right through you.' If you are feeling hungry, here's a pound of meat," and saying that, Monkey jammed his fist into her lower abdomen.

Rakshasi tumbled to the floor and began to moan. "Or how about a little taste of my toes?" Monkey roared, and thrust his foot down hard on her kidneys. Rakshasi let out a scream and began to roll across the floor. "Handsome Monkey King," she called out, "please spare my life!"

"I don't want your life," Monkey said. "I only want your fan."

"I'll give you the fan," Rakshasi moaned. "I'll give it to you! Only come out of my stomach!"

"First bring it out so I can see it," Monkey said. Rakshasi quietly ordered one of her maids to bring her palm leaf fan. Monkey turned himself back into a gnat and crawled up her throat. When he peered out from her mouth and saw the fan, he said, "Since I'm going to spare you, sister, I'll not come out through your rib cage, so you needn't worry. Just open your mouth three times." Rakshasi did as she was told and Monkey buzzed out, unnoticed, and landed on her fan. Rakshasi, of course, did not see him, and kept opening and closing her mouth. "Handsome Monkey King, please come out," she pleaded.

Monkey changed back to his true form, grabbed the fan, and said, "Here I am, sister, and thanks for the loan!"

Monkey rode his cloud back to the red gate. On seeing Monkey, Pigsy hollered, "Master, he's back—Monkey has come back!" Tripitaka and Sandy rushed out to greet Monkey. When they had all gone back inside, Monkey propped up the fan and said to the old man, "Is this the fan?"

"Yes, yes," the old man said, "that is it."

"Worthy disciple, you have performed a great service," Tripitaka said. "Tell us how you were able to snare this great treasure."

Showing great humility, Monkey explained how he had acquired the fan. He concluded by saying, "When we have crossed that Flaming Mountain, I am going to take the fan back to her."

Tripitaka was very pleased by Monkey's right attitude and conduct. After they had been served tea, they took leave of the old man and set off in the direction of Flaming Mountain.

When they had traveled some forty miles, the heat became so intense that they were forced to stop. "My feet are starting to roast," Sandy said. "My trotters are beginning to blister," Pigsy chimed in. "Master," Monkey said, "you'd better dismount. Don't anyone move, I'm going to use the fan to put out this fire. After the wind and rain have cooled the ground, we will be able to cross the mountain."

Monkey took out his fan and, raising it high, walked toward the flames and began to fan. Although he was fanning with all his might, instead of diminishing, the flames kept growing. With each wave of his fan the fire billowed higher and higher. By the third wave of the fan the fire had leaped to a height of ten thousand feet and was beginning to rumble and roar. Monkey began to retreat, but all the hairs on his thigh were already burnt. "Go back! Go back!" he shouted to the others. "The fire is coming this way!"

18

The Bull Demon's Wife

*T*RIPITAKA climbed back on his horse and galloped back toward the East, with the others close behind. They retreated twenty miles before stopping for a rest. "What happened?" Tripitaka said.

"I've been fooled!" Monkey cried. "Yes, I've been fooled. That dirty woman tricked me."

"What are we to do now?" Tripitaka sobbed.

"Hey, Brother," Pigsy said to Monkey, "you like to brag that nothing can hurt you, neither thunder nor fire, so what happened to you back there?"

"You idiot!" Monkey exclaimed. "You just don't understand anything. In the past I was able to prepare myself, so I wasn't hurt. Today I was trying to put out the fire and didn't make any flame-avoiding spells; that's how come I got singed."

"What will we do?" Sandy said. "I don't see how we'll ever get through the fire now."

"We'll have to try and go around it," Pigsy said.

"And where would that take us?" Tripitaka asked.

"Well," Pigsy said, "either East, South, or North."

"But in which direction are the scriptures?" Tripitaka said.

"In the West," Pigsy said.

"Then that's where we're going," Tripitaka commanded.

"This is some dilemma," Sandy said. "Where there are scriptures, there's fire; where there's no fire, there are no scriptures."

While they were going back and forth in this fashion,

they heard a voice that seemed to come out of nowhere. "Don't fret, Great Sage. Have something to eat before you decide what to do next." They turned to see an old man in a full wind-blown cape, wearing a hat in the shape of a half-moon and hobnailed boots, and holding a dragon-headed cane. Standing beside him was a hawk-beaked demon with broad fishlike cheeks. On its head was balanced a copper pot filled with steaming cakes, cooked millet, and rice.

The old man bowed. "I am the local god of Flaming Mountain. When I heard that the Great Sage had been stymied, and that the T'ang monk could not proceed on his holy mission, I came to present you with a meal."

"Never mind about food," Monkey said. "What we need is to have those fires extinguished."

"For that you must borrow Rakshasi's fan."

Monkey walked over and picked up the fan he had used on the fire. "This was supposed to be the fan, but when I waved it at the fire, it grew hotter and fiercer, instead of going out, as it was supposed to do."

The local god laughed. "You've been fooled. This is not the real fan."

"I know that," Monkey said. "But how do I get the real one?"

The local god bowed again and smiled. "If you want to borrow the real fan, you will have to find the Mighty King. Now please take a seat and allow me to serve you."

After they had eaten, the local god said, "The Mighty King is the Bull Demon King."

"Are you saying that this mountain was set ablaze by the Bull Demon King?"

"No, no," the local god said. "I will tell you why this mountain is burning, but only if you promise not to be angry."

"Speak up!" Monkey said. "You have my promise."

The local god gulped and said, "The Great Sage set this mountain on fire."

"What nonsense! I've never set eyes on this mountain before today. Are you calling me an arsonist?"

"I'm sure you don't recognize me," the local god said. "You see, this mountain was not always here. Five hundred years ago, when you caused great havoc in Heaven and were placed in the custody of Lao-tzu, I was then a Taoist worker in charge of the brazier in the Tushita Palace. Do you recall how you escaped from the crucible of Eight Trigrams, kicking over the elixir oven in the process? Well, some of the bricks that were still on fire fell down on this spot and became transformed into Flaming Mountain. Lao-tzu was so angry with me that he banished me to this mountain and made me its local spirit."

"So that explains your getup," Pigsy said. "You're a Taoist turned local deity."

Monkey was skeptical. "Tell me again why you think I need to fight the Mighty King."

"The Mighty King," the local god began, "just happens to be the husband of Rakshasi, but he left these parts some time ago and is now living at the Cloud-Touching Cave in the Mountain of Gathering Thunder. The cave master there was a fox king who had lived for ten thousand years. When he passed away he left behind a daughter named Princess Jade Countenance, who inherited a vast fortune that she did not know how to manage. When she learned about the Bull Demon King and his enormous magical powers, she offered to share her fortune if he would come and protect her. That is why the Bull Demon King no longer resides here. He abandoned Rakshasi and moved in with Princess Jade Countenance, and has not been back since. Only by finding him will the Great Sage stand a chance of borrowing the real magic fan. If you can persuade him to lend it to you, you will be able to accomplish three important deeds. One, your Master will be able to continue his journey; two, the land will be restored, to the benefit of all the people here; and three, I will obtain a pardon and return to Lao-tzu and the Taoist Patriarchy."

"Where is this Mountain of Gathering Thunder located, and how far is it from here?" Monkey asked.

"Due south, about three thousand miles," the local god replied.

Monkey told Pigsy and Sandy to look after the Master. Giving himself a shake, he somersaulted onto his cloud and disappeared. It took him less than an hour to arrive at the summit of the craggy peak. After having a careful look around, he started down the pointy summit. Monkey was not quite certain which direction to head in, when all at once a young maiden holding an orchid emerged from the edge of a pine grove. She was dressed in turquoise silk and wore her jet black hair in a bun. Her green eyes shone like jade pools. She seemed to Monkey to be a cloud-driven, rain-scented goddess, and he wondered what she was doing in this strange setting.

Monkey stepped forward and bowed. "Lady Bodhisattva, where are you headed?" The girl raised her head and noticed Monkey for the first time. She trembled at the sight of him. "Who are you?" she asked, "and where do you come from?"

Monkey thought fast. "If I tell her that I am going to the West to fetch scriptures and that I need to borrow the fan, she might become suspicious. In fact, she might even be related to the Bull Demon." He said, "This is my first visit to this region. Please tell me, is this the Mountain of Gathering Thunder? I fear that I may have gotten lost."

公主百花羞

The Bull Demon's consort, Princess Jade Countenance

"This is the Mountain of Gathering Thunder," the girl said.

"In that case, perhaps you can tell me how to find the Cloud-Touching Cave."

"Why do you wish to find it?"

"I have been sent by the Princess Iron Fan of the Palm Leaf Cave at Jade Cloud Mountain to fetch the Bull Demon King."

The girl's mouth dropped open, and her face turned crimson. "That horrid witch!" she screamed. "It has been scarcely two years since the Bull Demon and I have been together. In that time he has sent her countless jewels and precious stones, not to mention bolts of silk and satin. He provides her with allotments of firewood and rice. You'd think she'd be satisfied, but no, now that shameless demoness wants him back."

Monkey knew, long before her harangue was finished, that this was the Princess Jade Countenance. Raising his cudgel in the air, he exclaimed, "You heartless one, you buy a husband with your dowry, and you dare call another shameless. You are the one without shame or honor!"

The Princess was so terrified by Monkey's outburst that her soul nearly departed from her body. Shaking from head to foot, she turned and began to run through the pine forest. Monkey was close on her heels, shouting at the top of his lungs. When they arrived at the entrance of the Cloud-Touching Cave, the girl dashed inside the open door and closed it behind her. Monkey put his cudgel away and began to ponder his next move.

Her heart pounding wildly, the girl ran into the library, where the Bull Demon King was studying a book on alchemy. She fell at his feet, and wailing, began clawing at her cheeks in despair. The Bull Demon King tried to comfort her, but the more he tried to soothe her, the more wretched she became.

"You're killing me, that's what you're doing, you're killing me, you demon monster, you bellowing simpleton."

"Perhaps I said something I shouldn't have? . . ."

"I brought you here to look after me and protect me because I lost my parents. I thought you were a hero, strong, powerful, and fearless—but no, you're a henpecked nitwit!"

"But why do you say I'm killing you?" the Bull Demon asked, trying to reason with his concubine.

"I was out for a leisurely stroll just now, picking orchids and listening to the songs of the birds, when I was confronted by a hairy-faced monk with the visage of a thunder god. He bowed and then began asking me one question after another. It turns out he's been sent here to fetch you for the Princess Iron Fan. When I screamed at him what a witch Rakshasi was, he suddenly turned on me, raising a monstrous weapon as if to strike me, and I narrowly escaped with my life. If I hadn't taken you in, none of this would have happened!"

The Bull Demon King tried to pacify her. "My sweetness," he said, "you know I have no secrets from you. The Palm Leaf Cave is an obscure sanctuary known for its purity and high ideals. My wife Rakshasi has practiced austerities since her youth and is now an immortal traveling on the One Path. Her household is so strict that she doesn't keep a single page boy. So how could she send a man with the face of a thunder god to speak on her behalf? That hairy-faced monk must be a fiend who is using her name to search for me. I had better go out there and have a look."

The Bull Demon King walked out of the library and into the main hall, where he put on his armor and took up his weapon. Then he strode out of the cave, shouting, "Where are you, fiendish devil? Step forward and account for yourself!"

Monkey collected himself, tidied his clothes, and bowed

to the Bull Demon. The Bull Demon gave a start. "Aren't you the Great Sage, Equal of Heaven?" he asked.

"Yes, indeed," Monkey said. "Just a moment ago I was having an interesting conversation with your charming wife."

"Don't try that on me," the Bull Demon said. "The last I heard, you were chased out of Heaven and pinned beneath the Mountain of the Five Phases by the Buddha. Now all at once you show up at my door to insult and terrify my mistress."

Monkey laughed self-consciously. "I had no idea the girl I was questioning was the concubine of the formidable Bull Demon. When she scolded me, I'm afraid I lost my temper. I didn't mean any harm. I beg your forgiveness."

"I'll spare you this time," the Bull Demon said.

"Oh, thank you," Monkey said. "I'm overwhelmed by your kindness and understanding. However, there is one other matter I must trouble you with. I beg your help. . . ."

"You smart-mouthed ape! Don't you know there are limits? I told you I would spare your life, but instead of making yourself scarce, you start pestering me. What do you mean, my help?"

"I'll tell you the truth," Monkey said. "I'm accompanying a scripture-seeking pilgrim to the West, on commission from the Bodhisattva Kuan-yin. We got as far as the Flaming Mountain, where we were stopped in our tracks. The natives of that region informed us that the immortal Rakshasi has a palm leaf in her possession that could extinguish the fires, but she has refused to lend it to me. That's why I have come to you, hoping you would intercede on our behalf and secure us the loan of this magical fan, that we might resume our holy mission. As soon as we have crossed the Flaming Mountain I shall return it to you."

The Bull Demon flew into a rage. He had been gnashing

his steely teeth while Monkey spoke, and now he roared, "So it's the fan you want. First you torment my wife, and now you terrorize my mistress. There's a saying, 'Don't push a man's wife around, don't run his concubine into the ground.' You outrageous dunce!" the Bull Demon concluded as he raised his iron mace in the air.

"If you want to strike me, go ahead, but I've only come to borrow your treasure, not to engage you in combat."

"If you can survive three rounds with me," the Bull Demon roared, "I'll make my wife lend it to you, but if not, I will kill you and have my revenge."

"Right you are, great Demon," Monkey said. "Let's see if your mace is the equal of Monkey's cudgel."

The three rounds passed to ten and then one hundred, with neither one gaining a noticeable advantage. At that moment they heard a voice resounding from one of the mountain peaks: "Courageous Bull Demon, my Master invites you to honor him with your presence at a banquet."

On hearing this, the Bull Demon warded off the next blow of Monkey's cudgel and said, "Monkey, we must postpone our battle for the time being so that I can attend the banquet of a friend." With that he dropped down from his cloud and returned to his cave. "My dearest," he said to Princess Jade Countenance, "I've given that Monkey fiend a good licking; he won't be back. You can relax and forget about him."

After removing his armor, he put on a duck-green silk jacket, walked outside, and mounted his water-cleaving, golden-eyed steed. Ordering his underlings to guard the door, he zoomed off toward the northwest, flying between earthly mist and the Heavenly clouds.

❦

Standing on a summit, Monkey watched his adversary leave as he thought to himself, "Who could have sent for the Bull Demon, and where is the banquet being held? I think I'll follow along and find out." Shaking himself and changing into a cool breeze, he followed in the Bull Demon's tracks. Before Monkey was able to catch up, they came to a mountain where the demon suddenly disappeared. Changing back to his true form, Monkey walked along until he came to a lagoon, beside which stood a stone tablet with the inscription: Craggy Rock Mountain, Emerald Lagoon. "This is surely where that Bull Demon went," Monkey thought. "Since underwater spirits are lesser dragons, he must have changed himself into a turtle or fish." Monkey changed himself into a thirty-six-pound crab and plopped into the water, sinking quickly to the bottom.

Monkey found himself staring at a finely carved ornamental archway, to which was tethered the water-cleaving, golden-eyed steed of the Bull Demon. He was surprised to find that the region beyond was waterless. Monkey scuttled through the archway, looking from side to side and following the sound of music that was coming from a palace in the distance. When he approached the gated entrance he saw the Bull Demon King in the seat of honor, with several dragon spirits on either side. Facing him was an ancient dragon spirit, surrounded and attended by scores of dragon wives, daughters, sons, grandparents, and grandchildren. They were feasting and merrily toasting one another, when Monkey, in his crab form, scuttled straight in the direction of the Bull Demon King. The ancient dragon, the first to spot Monkey, ordered his immediate arrest. "Catch that vagrant crab!" he exclaimed. "How dare you barge in here and disgrace this hall with your presence? Speak up, or we will put you to death."

Disguising his voice, Monkey cried, "Spare me! Spare me!"

"Where are you from, and what are you doing here?" the ancient dragon demanded to know.

"Kindly noble," Monkey said, "I have lived since birth in this lagoon, dwelling in cliffs and coves. In recent years I have stretched my territory a bit and have earned the title Sidewise-Scuttling Knight in Armor, but having dragged my days through mud and grass, I am ignorant of the social graces. Please forgive me if in my ignorance I have offended Your Majesty."

All the attending spirits rose together. Bowing to the ancient dragon, they said, "This is the first time that the Sidewise-Scuttling Knight in Armor has entered the Royal Palace. Since he doesn't understand royal etiquette, we beg your Excellency to pardon him."

The ancient dragon thanked the spirits and ordered that the crab be released and removed from the palace.

Once outside the gateway, Monkey thought to himself, "That demon will soon be in his cups. Even if I do wait for him here, it probably won't do me any good. Why don't I assume his appearance, steal his steed, and go deceive Rakshasi? That would be a much better move than trying to reason with that drunken fool."

Monkey changed himself back to his true form and untied the reins of the golden-eyed beast. Leaping onto the carved saddle, he rode straight out of the lagoon. When he came to the surface, he transformed himself again, this time into an exact likeness of the Demon Bull King, and headed straight for the Palm Leaf Cave on Jade Cloud Mountain.

"Open up! Open up!" he bellowed, impersonating the voice of the Bull Demon. The two maidens who were standing guard inside the cave entrance immediately swung open the gates. They rushed inside at once to announce that the Bull Demon King had come home. Rakshasi nervously tidied her hair, and came rushing out to greet her husband. She took his hand and they walked back inside, while the maidens retired to make tea and prepare food.

"My good lady," said the deceiving Monkey, "it's been too long!"

"The Great King has become partial to his concubine and has abandoned his wife. So tell me, what is the name of the breeze that has blown you back home?"

"Abandon you? Never! Only my household duties have kept me away. I've come now to tell you that an immortal monkey is traveling with a T'ang monk, and they are headed in this direction. I fear that he will come looking for your fan. He's a loathsome beast and a trouble-making fiend. Should he show up, send for me at once and I will make short work of him."

On hearing this, Rakshasi burst into tears. "Your Majesty," she sobbed, resting her head on his shoulder, "remember the proverb that says, 'A man without a wife stands to lose everything, but a woman without a husband has nothing to gain.' That dirty monkey has been here already. He nearly killed me."

"When was he here?"

"He's still here, so far as I know. He came yesterday to borrow my fan. I blew him away, but he came right back, this time having acquired wind-arresting magic. Next he turned himself into a bug and crept inside my stomach and proceeded to pummel my insides, until I agreed to give him the fan."

"Horrors!" Monkey screeched, feigning outrage. "My dearest, how could you give our treasure to that hideous fiend?"

Rakshasi laughed. "Don't worry, your lordship, it was a fake."

"Where is the real fan, then?"

Rakshasi demurred. "You needn't be troubled, King, it is safe with me. Now that you are at my side nothing can go wrong." While Rakshasi spoke, the wine she had ordered was brought in. Raising her glass, she said, "Because of his new heartthrob, the King has nearly forgotten his wife. Let us have some homemade wine together, to toast your return."

Monkey had no choice but to comply. "Let the first sip be yours," he said. "You have looked after our property and kept our home. I am deeply grateful for all you have done."

"There is an old proverb," Rakshasi said: " 'The wife manages, but the husband provides.' There is no reason for you to thank me."

As they spoke, the maidens brought in bowls of fruit and meat and placed them between Rakshasi and her King. Monkey ate a piece of fruit only, keeping to his vegetarian vow, but he could not refuse Rakshasi's insistence that they drink more wine. Rakshasi soon began to snuggle up to Monkey, taking his hand in hers. It wasn't long before they were drinking out of the same goblet. Monkey was afraid he would also become a little tipsy if he wasn't careful. "My dearest," he said, "where have you put the real fan? I worry that that monkey fiend will show up and trick you again."

Rakshasi giggled, and pulled the fan out of her mouth. "Here it is," she said, handing it over. Monkey was startled at its size, for it was no bigger than an apricot leaf. Staring at the fan, he thought to himself, "How could a tiny thing like this put out a mountain of flame? Could it be that this is another phony fan?"

Seeing that his thoughts were taking him away from her, Rakshasi put her cheek against his and purred, "My darling, put the fan away and have another goblet of wine. There is nothing to worry about now."

Completely mesmerized by the fan, and forgetting himself, Monkey asked, "How could something this tiny put out eight hundred miles of roaring flames?"

Rakshasi had had too much to drink to be suspicious. "I don't know what that Jade Princess has been doing to you in the two years you have been away from me, but whatever it is, it has caused you to lose your memory. Don't you remember, first you place your left thumb on the seventh red thread attached to the fan's handle, then you utter the magic words *Hui-hsu-ho-hsi-hsi-ch'ui-hu*, and immediately it will grow to twelve feet. After that you can do any change you like. Even if faced with eighty thousand miles of flame, this fan would extinguish them with a single wave."

With the fan in his hand, Monkey pretended to be wiping his face, while he stuck it in his mouth. Then he gave himself a shake and resumed his natural form. "Look again, Rakshasi," he teased, "aren't you ashamed at the way you've carried on with me, you hussy?" Rakshasi was so overcome with embarrassment and shame that she fell to the floor and began to kick and scream. "Oh, I could die! I could die!" she sobbed.

Monkey walked out of the cave and mounted his cloud. Anxious to try out the fan, he spat it into his hand, and after marveling for a moment over his feat in obtaining it, he pressed the seventh red thread with his left thumb and recited the magic incantation, *Hui-hsu-ho-hsi-hsi-ch'ui-hu*. It grew at once to a length of twelve feet. Looking closely, he was aware that it was beginning to glow with an auspicious light, to emanate a sacred aura, while the thirty-six threads of the handle formed an intricate trellis pattern. It was only then that Monkey realized that he knew the formula to make the fan grow, but not the one to shrink it. He held the fan tight to his body while he cruised toward his destination, careful not to lose his grip on the precious object.

19

Bull Demon Wins the Day

WHEN the banquet and festivities at the Emerald Lagoon had finally come to an end, the Bull Demon King went outside and found that his golden-eyed steed was missing. The ancient dragon king summoned all the spirits from the banquet and demanded to know who had stolen the Bull Demon's steed. The spirits all knelt before the ancient Dragon King as they replied, "None of us would ever dare steal that beast. We were at the banquet the whole time, serving food, presenting the various wines, making music and singing. None of us left the banquet hall the entire time."

"Of course!" the ancient exclaimed. "None of our family would ever dare do such a thing. That I know. But have there been any strangers here tonight?"

"Shortly after the festivities began," they said, "that crab spirit came in. He was certainly a stranger."

On hearing this the Bull Demon realized at once what had happened. "It was that monkey demon, Great Sage, Equal of Heaven," he said.

"Do you mean the Great Sage who made havoc in Heaven?" they asked.

"The very one," the Bull Demon replied. "It was he who turned himself into a crab and then stole my steed. I'm sure he's gone back to Palm Leaf Cave to try to wangle that fan away from Rakshasi."

Without another word, the Bull Demon cleaved the waters and rode a cloud straight to the Palm Leaf Cave. The golden-eyed beast was tethered at the gate, and inside he could hear his wife wailing. He pushed open the door and shouted, "Where has the monkey demon gone, or is he still here on the premises?" The maidens all fell to their knees, exclaiming, "Sire, you have returned!" Rakshasi came charging out of the chamber where she had dishonored herself. Enough time had passed for her shame to have turned to anger. "You incorrigible reprobate!" she screamed at her husband, pounding his chest with her fists. "How many times have I been deceived because of you!"

Grinding his teeth, the Bull Demon said, "Which way did he go? Just tell me which way he went!"

"How should I know?" Rakshasi cried, pulling at her hair. "He resumed his old, wicked form and flew away with my fan."

"I'll leave at once to catch that hateful ape and return with your fan," shouted the King. "I'll skin him alive, I'll break every bone in his body, I'll gouge out his heart and liver and serve them to you on a platter!" He turned from Rakshasi and called for his weapons. "But your weapons are no longer here," the attendants said.

"In that case bring me Rakshasi's weapons!" Taking off his duck-green silk jacket and fastening his inner jacket tightly about his body, he seized the two steel-bladed treasure swords, one in each hand, and took off in pursuit of Monkey.

It wasn't long before the Bull Demon King came in sight of the Great Sage. From his cloud he spotted Monkey walking along with the magic fan on his shoulder. "Not only is he in possession of the fan," the Bull Demon muttered to himself, "but he's learned the magic that makes it work. If I were to challenge him now, he would give one wave of that fan and send me flying eight thousand miles away!"

While remaining suspended on the cloud over Monkey's head, the Bull Demon remembered that Tripitaka was traveling with two other disciples, Pigsy and Sandy, both of whom he was acquainted with. "I remember their appearances well enough to take on one of their forms," he thought, "and besides, that monkey is so full of himself right now that he has surely thrown all caution to the winds. I'll take the form of Pigsy, and then we will see."

Monkey was startled to see Pigsy walking along in his direction. "Elder Brother, it's me," the Bull Demon called out, in his best imitation of Pigsy's voice.

Monkey was feeling too exultant over his triumph to notice any discrepancies in Pigsy's getup and general appearance. As the saying goes, 'A cat that has won a fight is more pleased with himself than a tiger.' "Brother, what are you doing here?" he asked.

"You've been away so long that Master was afraid you had been subdued by the Bull Demon. He sent me out to look for you."

"You needn't have troubled yourself," Monkey chuckled. "As you can see, I have the magic fan." After Monkey had told him of his conquest in full detail, the Bull Demon said, "Elder Brother, you won a hard-fought battle. You must be exhausted. Let me carry that fan for you."

Without so much as a second thought, Monkey handed over the fan. The Bull Demon not only knew how to make the fan grow, but also the magic spell needed to make it shrink. Changing back to his true form, he bellowed, "What do you see now, you foolhardy simp?"

174

Monkey stamped his feet and, with a cry of anguish, said, "After all these years of hunting wild geese, a gosling has pecked out my eye!" Whipping out his cudgel, he struck at the Bull Demon's head, but the demon dodged the blow and waved at Monkey with the fan. To his great surprise nothing happened. He had forgotten that the Great Sage had acquired wind-arresting magic, for when Monkey had turned himself into a gnat to enter Rakshasi's stomach, he had first swallowed the pill, which had made his skin, bones, and viscera so solid and hard that no matter how strenuously the Bull Demon fanned he could not budge old Monkey.

Horrified and in a fury, the Bull Demon put the fan in his mouth and came charging after Monkey, wielding his two swords. They were soon whirling in midair. Monkey belched out a colored fog to conceal himself, but the Bull Demon spat out penetrating white rays to dispel it. Thundering and crashing, cursing and bellowing, the Earth and the Heavens were soon clouded in dust, and the flying stones and debris soon scattered the local spirits, ghosts, and deities.

Tripitaka was seated by the side of the road, quietly enduring the insufferable heat and conversing with the local spirit. "Just how powerful is the Bull Demon King?" he asked.

"His magic is great, and his dharma powers are unlimited," the local spirit said. "I would say that he is a match for the Great Sage."

"Monkey is an outstanding cloud-soarer," Tripitaka said. "He can travel two thousand miles in a trice. I wonder why he has been gone so long. He must be fighting the Bull Demon." Tripitaka called Sandy and Pigsy over and asked them, "Which of you will go to meet your elder brother? I fear that he is engaged in battle and needs our assistance. We must get that fan at any cost, so we can cross the mountain and resume our mission."

"I would like to go," Pigsy said, "but I don't know the way to Thunder Mountain."

"I know the way," the local spirit said, "and I will be happy to show you, if Sandy will stay here and look after the Master."

Tripitaka was very pleased. Pigsy tightened the belt over his tunic and took up his rake. Soon he and the local spirit were on a cloud and heading due east. They hadn't gone far when they began to hear shouting in the distance, accompanied by a loud, howling wind. They soon saw that the turbulence was being caused by Monkey and the Bull Demon. "What are you waiting for?" the local spirit said. "Jump into battle and help your brother!"

Clutching his rake and hollering, "Elder Brother, I'm here," Pigsy leapt into the fray. "You filthy bag of blood," he cried, "you dirty demonic fiend!" With that Pigsy began showering blows on the head and body of the Bull Demon as if possessed. Inspired by Pigsy, Monkey redoubled his efforts, and the Bull Demon, sensing defeat, began to flee. But he quickly found his way blocked by the local spirit and his ghost brigade. "King Powerful," the local spirit addressed him, "these are disciples of the monk Tripitaka, who is journeying to the West to seek scriptures. He is being protected by the Three Worlds, and the Ten Directions are supporting him. Lend them your fan at once, that he may blow out the flames and continue on his way. Otherwise Heaven will hold you culpable and you will certainly be executed."

"You are being unreasonable, local spirit," the Bull Demon said. "This foul ape has bullied my mistress and shamed my wife. Leave him to me, for I would like to swallow him whole and turn him to shit to feed the dogs. There is no way I will turn my fan over to him."

This was all the provocation Monkey and Pigsy needed. They came roaring after the Bull Demon, cursing and growling. The Demon King gnashed his teeth and met the attack of his two adversaries. This time the fight lasted throughout the night. By morning they had reached the entrance of Cloud-Touching Cave. Everyone inside the cave was aroused by the deafening din they were making, and Princess Jade Countenance ordered the maids to investigate the racket.

"It's our Master," they reported. "He's fighting the one with the thunder-god visage and also another monk with a long snout and huge ears. Also, hovering close by is the local spirit of Flaming Mountain, with all his minions."

When she heard this, Princess Jade Countenance summoned her troops into battle. Grabbing their lances and waving their swords, they came charging out the gate. "Great King, we are here to assist you!"

Overwhelmed by the screaming militia, Pigsy turned tail and fled in defeat, trailing his rake behind him, while Monkey, with a single somersault, jumped free of the encircling soldiers.

The battle won, the Bull Demon and his army returned to their cave and shut the door firmly behind them.

20

Putting Out the Fire

*M*ONKEY said to his companions, "I'm beginning to think we've met our match. When you came to help me last night we had already fought through the entire afternoon. In all that time he didn't show any signs of tiring. Not only that, but that little band of fiends that attacked us just now are a tough lot. Now the doors of his cave are shut tight and he won't come out. What are we to do?"

"Elder Brother," Pigsy said, "you left our Master yesterday morning, but you didn't start fighting with the demon until yesterday afternoon. That leaves six hours unaccounted for. What were you doing all that time?"

"Well," Monkey said, "I came directly to this mountain, where I ran into the demon's concubine, Princess Jade Countenance. I gave her a scare before I realized who she was. She fled to her cave and sent her Bull Demon after me. We swapped a few insults and then started fighting. A couple of hours went by, and then he was invited to a banquet. I trailed him to a lagoon and changed into a crab. Then I stole his steed, took on his appearance, and returned to Palm Leaf Cave, where I tricked Rakshasi into giving me the fan. When I left her I tried to work the fan. I had learned how to enlarge it, but not how to shrink it. As I was journeying back with it, the Demon Bull, assuming your likeness, got the fan back from me. That's what happened during those hours."

"As the saying goes, 'It's just like the boatload of bean curd. It fell in the river and got fished out of the lake! Easy coming in, no trouble going out.' But how will we ever get our Master over that mountain without the fan? It looks like we're going to have to find a detour."

"Don't lose heart or reason," the local spirit warned Pigsy and Monkey. "If you leave the true path, you'll never cultivate right conduct. The ancients never traveled the byways or looked for shortcuts. Think of your Master, desperately sitting on the main road, waiting for your success."

Monkey jumped up, excited. "Exactly!" he cried. And turning to Pigsy, he said, "Don't talk nonsense, idiot. The local spirit is right. We must persevere."

In an instant the local spirit had reassembled his ghost brigade. Following Monkey and Pigsy, they stormed the cave entrance, crashing it to the ground. The Bull Demon came charging out to meet them, and soon they were chasing one another among the clouds, battling with the same fury that had taken them through the night. This time the local spirit's army was able to trounce the Bull Demon's legions. But the Bull Demon did not give up easily. Seeing that the fight was going against him, he worked his way back to the cave. But this time he was met by the local spirit and his ghost battalion. "Halt, King Powerful!" the local spirit commanded. "This time we have you stopped!" The Bull Demon began to retreat, only to see Monkey and Pigsy flying down on him. Tearing off his helmet and armor and throwing down his mace, he shook himself, turned into a swan, and flew away.

Monkey laughed to himself, and said, "Hey, Pigsy, that bull demon is gone." Pigsy had no idea what had happened, nor did the local spirit or the ghost soldiers. They were staring this way and that, their eyes traveling up and down the mountain.

Monkey pointed with his finger. "Isn't that him flying up there?"

"That's a swan," Pigsy replied.

"No," Monkey said, "it's a transformation of the bull."

"What do we do now?" the local spirit asked.

"Only one thing to do," said Monkey. "Take your troops inside that den and clean out all the demons. This will cut off the Bull Demon's retreat, and with nowhere to go he'll have to match transformations with old Monkey."

Monkey put away his cudgel, gave himself a shake, and turned into a vulture. He flew through the clouds, set his wings, and came hurtling down on the swan, hoping to seize its neck and peck out its eyes. The Bull Demon knew the vulture was a transformation and, flapping his wings, changed into a golden eagle and attacked the vulture. Monkey quickly turned into a black phoenix and went flying after the eagle. The Bull King was too fast for him: changing this time into a white crane, he flew toward the South, crying loudly.

Monkey stopped short for a moment, considering, and then, shaking his feathers, changed into a scarlet phoenix and gave out a bloodcurdling cry. At the sight of the phoenix, the ruler of all birds and fowl, the white crane swooped down the cliff and with a beat of his wings turned into a musk deer, lazily grazing at the foot of the hill.

Monkey folded his wings and came diving down. The instant he touched the ground he turned into a ravenous tiger and came running after the deer. Terrified, the Bull Demon quickly changed into a spotted leopard and turned to challenge the tiger. Seeing his predicament, Monkey faced the wind and with a single shake became a golden-eyed lion, with a roar like thunder and a head of bronze stamped with an iron brow. Spinning around, he pounced on the leopard, but in that instant the Bull Demon had changed into a monstrous bear and began chasing the lion. Monkey rolled over on the ground and

SHAMBHALA PUBLICATIONS, INC.

Mailing List
P.O. Box 308, Back Bay Annex
Boston, Massachusetts   02117

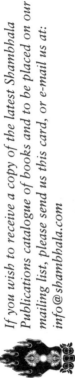

If you wish to receive a copy of the latest Shambhala Publications catalogue of books and to be placed on our mailing list, please send us this card, or e-mail us at: info@shambhala.com

PLEASE PRINT

Book in which this card was found

NAME _____

ADDRESS _____

CITY & STATE _____

ZIP OR POSTAL CODE _____ COUNTRY _____

                                                                  (if outside U.S.A.)

E-MAIL ADDRESS _____

became a serpent-trunked elephant, with tusks like bamboo shoots. He whipped his trunk around and tried to snare the bear. The Bull Demon gave an uproarious laugh and turned into his original form, a great white bull, with a head like a rugged mountain, eyes like twin beams of light, horns like iron pagodas, and teeth like sharp rows of swords. He was ten thousand feet in length from head to tail, and stood eight hundred feet above the ground.

"How now, miserable ape!" he bellowed from on high. But Monkey was not to be undone. Changing back to his true form, he took out his cudgel, straightened his back, and cried, "Grow!" In an instant he was one hundred thousand feet tall, with a head like Mount T'ai, eyes like the sun and moon, his mouth a bloody crimson pool, and his teeth like doors. Raising his cudgel on high, he brought it down on the bull's flinty head, sending sparks in ten directions. The bull roared and shook his gleaming horns and, kicking up mounds of dirt with his hooves, came charging after Monkey. The mountains began to shake, and the earth to tremble. It wasn't long before the deities surrounding that region came rushing forward in an attempt to hem the bull in. Monkey was encouraged by the sight of the Golden-Headed Guardian, the Six Gods of Darkness and the Six Gods of Light, and the Eighteen Guardians of the Faith. But the Bull Demon was undaunted. He kept whipping his body from side to side, lashing at the deities with his spiky tail.

Attacking him relentlessly from all sides, Monkey's allies soon wearied the bull. Finally he was brought to his knees, but he rolled over, changed back to his original form, and fled in the direction of the Palm Leaf Cave.

Monkey immediately reverted to his true form and, with the deities at his side, set off in hot pursuit. When the Bull Demon King reached the cave, he locked the door behind him and refused to come out. The deities quickly cast a protective net over Jade Cloud Mountain.

Monkey was about to attack the cave entrance when he heard shouting in the distance. He looked around to see Pigsy approaching, with the local spirit and the ghost soldiers close behind. When Monkey saw them, he shouted, "What happened at Cloud-Touching Cave?"

Pigsy called back, "I put an end to the mistress of that cave with one blow of my rake. When I stripped her, she turned out to be a white-faced fox, and her demons were all donkeys, mules, cows, badgers, foxes, raccoons, deers, goats, antelopes, and the like. They've all been dispatched, and we set fire to the cave."

"Why have you come here?" Monkey asked.

"The local spirit says he has another woman living here, so we've come back to make a clean sweep."

"Well done, brother! Congratulations! I was unable to best the old bull in a contest of transformations, but with the help of these deities we were able to rout him. But he has returned to his cave and won't come out. We have him surrounded, and I was just about to break down the doors when you came along."

"This must be Palm Leaf Cave, then," Pigsy said.

"Yes," Monkey said, "this is where Rakshasi lives."

"What are we waiting for?" Pigsy said. "Let's fight our way in and demand that he turn over the fan." Monkey could see that Pigsy's blood was still boiling from his last battle. He stepped aside and gave him the sign to go ahead. Raising his rake overhead, Pigsy unleashed a mighty blow on the door and sent it crashing.

The maids inside the door dashed into the chambers, screaming, "Your Majesty, the door has been demolished!" The Bull Demon King flew into a rage. He had just been telling Rakshasi about his encounter with Monkey. He took out the fan, spat on it, and handed it to his wife. "Cursed Monkey!" he bellowed. "Will this never end?"

"Great King," Rakshasi pleaded, "give the monkey the fan and have him call off his troops."

"It is no longer a question of the fan," the Bull Demon said. "It's gone way beyond that." Without another word of explanation, he put on his armor and took up his swords. When Pigsy saw him coming, he retreated a few steps to protect himself. They were now outside the doorway, and Monkey joined in the fight. Rising up on a gust of wind, the Bull Demon soared clear of the cave, with Monkey, Pigsy, the gods, the ghost soldiers, and the local spirit hot on his trail.

This time they fought over fifty rounds before the Bull Demon was forced to retreat. He fled to the North, where he quickly came up against the Diamond Guardian Diffusion of the Mysterious Demon Cave on Mount Wu-t'ai. "Where do you think you're going, bull monster? I have been commanded by the Lord Buddha to set up cosmic nets to capture you." When the Bull Demon looked back, he saw Monkey, Pigsy, and the others rushing toward him. In desperation, he turned and fled toward the South, where he was met by the Diamond Guardian Victorious of the Cave of Cool Purity on Mount Emei. The Guardian shouted, "I have been instructed by the Buddha to capture you. Don't move!" Terrified and exhausted, the Bull Demon fled East, where his path was blocked by the Diamond Guardian of Great Strength of Mo'er Cliff on Mount Sumeru. "Where are you going, Old Bull? Don't you know I have orders from the Buddha to arrest you?"

The Bull Demon King recoiled and fled toward the West, but this time he was met by the Diamond Guardian Ever-Abiding of Golden Brightness Ridge on Mount K'un-lun, who shouted, "Where do you think you're going? I've been instructed by the Buddha of the Great Thunderclap Monastery of the Western Heaven not to let you pass."

The Bull Demon mounted a cloud and attempted to flee skyward, but just then he saw Devaraja Li, the Pagoda Bearer, and Prince Natha, the Fish-Bellied Yaksha, as well as the Mighty Miracle God. "Stop at once!" they shouted. "We are here by mandate of the Jade Emperor to subjugate you." In desperation, the Bull Demon gave himself a shake and turned into a huge white bull, and with his iron hard horns tried to gore the devaraja, who stood his ground, sword in hand.

Just then Monkey appeared on the scene and was greeted by Prince Natha, who called out, "Forgive me for not greeting you properly, as I am in armor. We have been apprised of your situation and are here on orders from the Jade Emperor to lend you our assistance."

"So good of you," Monkey said, "but this monster's magical powers are tremendous. Look at him now! What can be done?"

"Not to worry, Great Sage. Just stand back and see how I deal with him." Shouting "Change!" the prince turned himself into a body with three heads and six arms. He leapt onto the bull's back and with one sweep of his monster-cleaving sword beheaded the Bull Demon. Sheathing his sword, Natha began walking toward Monkey when another head emerged from the torso of the bull and began to belch black smoke while its eyes shot out golden sparks. Prince Natha raised his sword and cut off the new head, but before the head fell to the ground, another head took its place. A dozen heads were cut off in this manner, and a dozen heads grew back.

As Monkey watched in amazement, Prince Natha took out his fire wheel and hung it on the bull's horns. He blew on the magic fire until it blazed so fiercely that the bull began to howl with pain, shaking his head and swishing his tail in an attempt to get free. He was about to transform himself again when Devaraja Li aimed his imp-reflecting mirror, making it impossible for the Bull Demon to either change himself or escape. "Spare my life!" he pleaded. "I am willing to submit to Buddhism."

"If you want to be spared," Prince Natha said, "hand over the fan."

"The fan is in the hands of my wife."

On hearing this, Prince Natha took his demon-binding rope, slipped it around the bull's neck and threaded it through his nostrils, and led him away. Monkey then assembled all the deities, gods, and spirits together, and with Pigsy at his side accompanied the prince to Palm Leaf Cave. When they reached the entrance the Demon Bull called out to his wife, "Please, dearest, bring out the fan and save my life."

As soon as she heard her husband's voice, Rakshasi removed her jewels and her fashionable garments. Slipping into a plain white robe worn by Buddhist nuns, she put her hair up like a Taoist priestess. Then she walked out, carrying the twelve-foot fan with both hands. At the sight of the gods she fell to her knees in terror and kowtowed, crying, "I beg the bodhisattvas to spare our lives. I present the fan to the Great Sage that he may achieve his mission and gain merit."

Monkey stepped forward and took the fan from her upraised arms. Mounting their auspicious clouds, they returned to the West.

Tripitaka and Sandy were alternately sitting and standing by the side of the road, growing more and more anxious, and wondering if the disciples would ever return. All at once portentous clouds began to fill the air, and the earth became illuminated with a blessed light, as the gods and divinities came floating down from the sky. Tripitaka was concerned, and said to Sandy, "What divine army is that coming our way?"

Sandy recognized them and replied, "Master, those are the four Great Diamond Guardians, the Golden-Headed Guardian, the Six Gods of Darkness and the Six Gods of Light, the Eighteen Guardians of Monasteries, plus other deities of the void. The one leading the bull is Prince Natha, and the one holding the mirror is Devaraja Li, the Pagoda Bearer. Pigsy is following Elder Brother, who appears to be carrying the fan. The others are all celestial guards."

On hearing this, Tripitaka put on his cape and Vairochana hat and, leading Sandy, went to welcome the gods and sages. "What virtue does this humble disciple possess that he should cause all you holy ones to come down to Earth?"

"Congratulations, holy monk!" the Four Great Diamond Guardians replied. "Your great task is nearly accomplished. We have been sent by Buddha to help. You must persevere and not slacken for a moment. The goal is in sight." Tripitaka kowtowed repeatedly while receiving his instructions.

Monkey took the fan in hand and stood facing the Flaming Mountain as he waved it with all his might. The flames went out at once, leaving a rosy glow in their wake. He fanned a second time, and a cool breeze began to stir. When he fanned the mountain for a third time, the sky became overcast and a gentle rain began to fall.

Tripitaka's mind was now set at rest. Master and disciples bowed and gave thanks to the Diamond Guardians, who returned to their mountain homes. The Six Cyclic Gods rose in the air to extend their continued protection, while the other deities returned to the void. The devaraja and the prince led the bull back to the Buddha, leaving only the local spirit to stand guard over Rakshasi. "Why have you been left behind?" Monkey asked Rakshasi. "Haven't I seen enough of you?"

Rakshasi fell to her knees. "I beg the Great Sage in his mercy to return my fan."

"What cheek!" Monkey screamed. "We've spared you your life, isn't that enough? By your brazen indifference you have forfeited the right to this fan. Why, when we cross over the mountain I plan to trade it in for something useful. Do you think after all this trouble that we would give it back? You'd better go home and get out of the rain."

Rakshasi bowed again and, holding back her tears, pleaded with Monkey. "The Great Sage said he would return the fan once the fire was out. It was only because I was anxious and fearful that I put you through all that trouble. Although we have not learned we have achieved human form. With our true bodies turned to the West we can never be willfully wicked again. I beg you to return the fan that I may live a new life in self-cultivation and the Truth."

The local spirit stepped forward. "Great Sage," he said, "why not find out from this woman how the flames can be permanently extinguished? Then you can return her fan and you will both be happy. In addition, this humble deity, who must remain in this region, will be able to help the people and live in peace. This would truly be a great kindness to me."

Monkey turned to Rakshasi and waited for her to speak. "Great Sage," she began, "if you would like these flames to be put out forever, you must fan them forty-nine times in succession. Then they will never start again."

Monkey held the fan in both hands, faced the mountain, and fanned forty-nine times. When he had finished, a torrential rain fell on the mountain. They could see that the rain was falling from a single black cloud, while the rest of the sky remained blue. No rain fell where they stood, but the downpour continued to drench the mountain, which soon turned the color of charcoal.

The following morning they put their luggage in order, saddled the white horse, and prepared to journey over the mountain. Monkey returned the fan to Rakshasi, saying, "If I didn't return your fan, people would say that I was incapable of keeping my word. You too must keep your word and not start any more trouble. I am sparing you because you have attained a human form."

Rakshasi took the fan from Monkey's hand and recited a spell that returned it to its original size. After placing it in her mouth, she bowed to Monkey and thanked him again, saying that she intended to become a recluse and practice self-cultivation. In time she attained to sainthood, and her name is now preserved in the Buddhist canons.

21

The Path Behind the Temple
and the Bottomless Boat

*B*ECAUSE of their successful attainment of the Fan of Pure
Yin, Tripitaka and his disciples had attained the condition
that brought water and fire into perfect equilibrium, and their
own natures had become pure and cool. They traveled leisurely now, with carefree spirits, and on the following day
they were able to cover a distance of eight hundred miles.

It was the time between late autumn and early winter. In
the villages the grains had all been harvested and stored. The
early morning frosts had begun to edge the ponds with ice.
The fading wisteria dangled over the ridges, while bamboo and
pine gleamed even greener in the morning mists. The vapors
of earth clung to the earth, while the vapors of Heaven rose
upward. Pure yin had now become yang.

The months passed as they continued their westward
trek. It wasn't only the change of seasons that made everything appear different, but the region itself was different. Everywhere they looked they saw gemlike flowers, magical
grasses, ancient cypresses, and hoary pines. Even the villages
were different here, the families devoting themselves to pious
works and the entertainment of priests. In the hills they saw
hermits preaching austerities, and in the woods they heard the
chanting of sutras.

Then one day they came in sight of a skyward-towering
spirit palace. They approached in silence, catching glimpses of

Hsuan-tsang, Sandy, Pigsy, and Monkey
reach the end of the road.

it through the dangling vines and moss-covered trees. When they reached the gate a young Taoist came out to greet them. "Are you not the scripture seekers from the Land of the East?" he asked. Tripitaka tidied his clothes and walked forward. As he stared at the young man's beautiful silk robe, he noticed that in one hand the latter held a jade-handled wisk, and hanging from his other wrist could be seen a sacred registry. Monkey whispered, "Master, this is the Golden-Crested Great Immortal of the Taoist Temple at the foot of Holy Spirit Mountain." Tripitaka immediately stepped forward and bowed. The immortal chuckled with delight. "So the T'ang monk has come at last. The Bodhisattva Kuan-yin misinformed me. She said I should expect you in two or three years' time. Year after year I have waited, but never was there any news. To find you here today before me is indeed a surprise."

Tripitaka pressed his palms together. "Thank you! Thank you! I am greatly indebted to the immortal's patience."

They were led inside, where they were served tea and a vegetarian meal. That evening they bathed, in order to purify themselves for the final ascent of their journey. The next morning Tripitaka changed into his brocaded cassock, and after placing his Vairochana hat on his head and taking his priestly staff in hand, he presented himself before the immortal in the main hall in order to take his leave. "You look so much better," the immortal said, looking Tripitaka up and down. "In one day your countenance has changed immeasurably. Today, as I look at you, you are a true son of Buddha." Tripitaka bowed and made to leave. "Just a moment," the immortal said. "Let me see you off."

"It's not really necessary," Tripitaka said, "Monkey knows the way."

"Monkey knows the way of the clouds, but not the way of the main-traveled road."

"What you say is so," Tripitaka agreed. "Perhaps you should take us to where the path begins."

The immortal led the way out back, for the path lay behind the temple. "Do you see that highest point," the immortal asked, pointing upward, "the one that is shrouded in luminous colors, and in folds of hallowed mist? That is Spirit Vulture Peak, the holy region of the Buddhist Patriarch." Tripitaka fell to his knees and began kowtowing.

"Master," Monkey warned, "there will be plenty of time for that later. If you start kowtowing now your head will be flat by the time we reach the summit."

They had not gone for more than five or six miles when they came upon a turbulent body of water that was at least eight miles across. "This can't be the right way," Tripitaka said. "Could the immortal have been mistaken? Look at how rough this water is! We can't possibly get across."

"This is the right way," Monkey said. "There's been no mistake. Look over there, isn't that a bridge?" They rushed over to have a look, but the bridge turned out to be a single log. Tripitaka was shaking all over as he said, "This is not a bridge for humans."

"But this is the way!" Monkey cried. "This is most truly the way!"

"This may be the way," Pigsy said, "but it's not the way I'm going."

Tripitaka assented. "It's too narrow and slippery."

"Stand back while I show you how it's done," said Monkey. Striding across the swaying bridge, Monkey was soon on the other side. "I made it!" he shouted. "Come on over!"

Tripitaka stood his ground, while Pigsy and Sandy bit their fingers and murmured, "Too hard! Too hard!"

Monkey dashed back over the log, and hollering, "Idiot!" at Pigsy, he tried to force him across. But Pigsy fell to the ground, crying, "Much too slippery! Much too slippery! Let me mount a cloud and ride over on the wind."

Monkey gave Pigsy a push. "Where do you think you are, that you can ride clouds and wind? Unless you can walk across this bridge you'll never become a buddha."

"Buddha or no buddha," Pigsy said, "I'm not crossing that bridge."

Monkey was about to grab hold of Pigsy again when Tripitaka turned and caught sight of someone punting a boat in their direction and shouting, "Ahoy! Ahoy!"

They froze in their tracks and stared at the boat as if it were a mirage. When the boat drew near Monkey saw that it had no bottom. Staring at the boatman with his fiery eyes, Monkey realized that it was the Conductor Buddha, also called the Light of the Banner. Keeping the buddha's identity to himself, he called out, "Over here, boatman, over here!"

When the boat pulled up to shore, Tripitaka looked down in disbelief, for although the boat was riding on the surface it had no bottom. "How can this bottomless boat take us across?" he exclaimed.

"You might think it can't," said the ferryman, "but this boat has carried many a soul to salvation."

Monkey pressed his palms together in thanks. When Tripitaka hesitated, Monkey said, "Don't worry, Master, this boat will never sink." Tripitaka began to grumble under his breath, but Monkey shoved him on board and forced the others to follow. The ferryman gently poled them away from the shore.

All at once they saw a body floating downstream. Tripitaka stared at the moving body in terrified disbelief. "Don't worry," Monkey said, "it's only you."

"It's you, it's you," Pigsy cried.

Clapping his hands, Sandy repeated, "It's you, Master, it's you!"

"Congratulations!" the boatman said. "It's you all right—and there you go!"

They soon reached the other shore. Tripitaka skipped lightly from the boat and jumped onto the bank. He had achieved transcendent wisdom and, having discarded his earthly body, had also cleansed his senses and become the master of his fate.

When they turned and looked back over the water, the boat had disappeared. Only then did Monkey tell them who the ferryman was. Tripitaka now realized what had happened. He began immediately to thank his disciples, but Monkey said, "We are each of us equally indebted to the other. If the Master had not accepted us as disciples, we would not have achieved merit, and if we had not protected the Master, he could not have transcended his mortal body."

Monkey then turned around and said, "Look, Master, at the shining scenery about us, magnificent flowers and joyful creatures everywhere. Is this not better than the places of illusion through which we have passed?"

Tripitaka continued to express his gratitude, and together they stepped lightheartedly along in the direction of the Holy Spirit Mountain, where they knew they would find the Great Thunderclap Monastery.

22

The Last Calamity

IT wasn't long before the pilgrims came at last to the monastery gates, where they were met by the Vajrapani of the Four Great Guardians, who proclaimed their welcome, saying, "His Reverence the sage monk has arrived."

"Yes, your disciple Hsuan-tsang has arrived," Tripitaka replied, but when he made a motion to enter through the gate, they hesitated, saying, "Kindly allow us to announce your arrival. Then you may enter."

The report was made from the outer gate all the way into the third interior gate, where it was received by divine monks who served at the Great Altar. They went at once to the Great Hero Treasure Hall to announce to the Holy Buddha that the scripture seeker from the T'ang Court had just arrived.

The Father Buddha was highly pleased and ordered the Eight Bodhisattvas, the Four Vajrapani Guardians, the Five Hundred Arhats, the Three Thousand Guardians, the Eleven Great Orbs, and the Eighteen Guardians of Monasteries to form two rows for the reception. Then, by official decree he summoned the T'ang monk Tripitaka to be shown in. Once again the word went back through all the gates, before Tripitaka and his entourage were commanded to proceed, observing carefully the prescribed rules of etiquette.

When the pilgrims reached the Great Hero Treasure Hall, they first prostrated themselves before the Buddha, and then bowed to his attendants on the right and on the left. This they repeated three times before kneeling before the Buddha and presenting their rescripts. The Buddha looked through each one before handing them back to Tripitaka, who touched his head to the ground, by acknowledgement, and said, "By order of the Emperor of T'ang, your disciple Hsuan-tsang has come to this holy monastery to beg you for the true scriptures for the redemption of all mankind. May the Lord Buddha in his grace grant me my wish, that I may quickly return to my native country."

After a long pause, the Buddha turned and called out the names of Ananda and Kashyapa, and commanded thus, "Take these four pilgrims and give them a room beneath the tower. First feed them; then open the doors of the treasury and select some scrolls from the thirty-five divisions of our three canons, which they will take with them to the Land of the East as a perpetual token of our grace."

When they were taken to their rooms beneath the tower, they saw spread before them a magnificent feast of foods unknown in the ordinary world. The deities in charge began first by serving Pigsy and Sandy, for the viands they were serving not only gave earthly enjoyment, granting health and longevity, but also transformed mortal substance into immortal flesh and bone.

When at last they had completed their feast, they were taken to the Treasury. When the doors were opened for them, they found themselves instantly bathed in beams of magic light. The scriptures lay in jeweled chests, their titles inscribed on red labels. After the scrolls had been sorted and arranged, they were duly handed over. Once they were properly examined and arranged, they were loaded on the white horse. Additional loads were made for Pigsy and Sandy, while Monkey led the steed. Tripitaka then took up his staff and, properly attired, led them once again to an audience with the Buddha.

The Buddha was seated on his lofty lotus throne. He

ordered the two Great Arhats to beat the cloudy stone gongs, summoning once more the congregation of the faithful. Soon celestial music was heard, while a hallowed mist loomed up in the sky.

After a report of the scripture titles was given, the four pilgrims put down their packs and tethered their horse. Pressing their palms together, they bowed before the Buddha, who was now ready to speak. He directed his gaze at Tripitaka. "The efficacy of these scriptures is immeasurable. They are not only a mirror of our faith, they are also the source of the Three Teachings. When you return with these and display them to the multitude, you must see that they are not lightly handled. No one should open a scroll who has not first fasted and bathed. Treasure them! Honor them! for in these scriptures are the secret mysteries for gaining immortality and comprehending the Tao, as well as the formulas for ten thousand transformations."

Tripitaka pressed his palms together and bowed three times with the greatest reverence before taking his leave. When they reached the monastery gates they thanked each of the sages again before making their departure.

After the Buddha had dismissed the assembly, Kuan-yin slipped out of the throng. Pressing her palms together before the Buddha, she said, "Many years ago I received a golden decree to find someone in China to fetch the holy scriptures. That pilgrim has now achieved his task, having taken fourteen years or five thousand and forty days to do so. He has received five thousand and forty-eight scrolls, and it would seem appropriate that he should complete his mission home in eight days; in that way the two figures would accord."

"A very good thought," the Buddha said. "You may see to it that a decree is issued to that effect." He then sent for the Eight Vajrapani Guardians and told them to exert their magic powers to transport the pilgrims back to the East. "When the scriptures have been deposited you are to bring them back here. All this must take exactly eight days, so as to fulfill the perfect canonical number of five thousand and forty-eight."

The Guardians at once caught up with the pilgrims and said, "Scripture takers, follow us!" Immediately they were carried skyward, where they were borne aloft on a magic cloud.

The Guardians of the Five Quarters, the Sentinels of the Four Watches, the Six Cyclic Gods, the Eighteen Guardians of Monasteries, and all the other divinities who had protected Tripitaka during his long journey now appeared before the Bodhisattva Kuan-yin and made their reports. "Now that the Bodhisattva has returned the Buddha's golden decree, we, your disciples, wish to submit the dharma decree under which you placed us to give secret protection to the T'ang monk."

The Bodhisattva was highly pleased. "You have my permission," she said. "Please tell me, how did the pilgrims discharge themselves during their long journey?"

"They demonstrated the greatest devotion and determination," replied the deities, "a fact that we are sure has not escaped your omniscient attention. We have made a complete record of this journey, and would like to present to you our registry."

The Bodhisattva read through the registry of ordeals. When she had finished, she said, "According to our faith, nine times nine is the crucial number by which one returns to immortality. Tripitaka has gone through eighty ordeals, which means he has fallen one short of the crucial number." Turning to one of the Guardians, she said, "Catch up to the Vajrapanis and have them arrange one final calamity."

Suddenly, without warning, the wind that was carrying the four pilgrims was retrieved, and they came crashing to the ground. Tripitaka was terribly frightened to find himself standing once again on profane ground, but Pigsy roared with laughter. "Isn't this a case of more haste, less speed?" he said.

Sandy said, "They must have thought we needed a rest."

"As the proverb goes," Monkey added, " 'Sit on the beach for ten days, shoot nine rapids on the following.' "

"Stop matching wits," Tripitaka scolded, "and let's find out where we are."

"I know this place, Master," Sandy said. "The sound of the water makes me feel at home."

"In that case," Monkey said, "it must be the River of Flowing Sands."

"Not at all," Sandy replied. "This is the Heaven-Flowing River."

"Monkey," Tripitaka commanded, "you had better go up and take a look."

Monkey leapt into the air and, shading his eyes with one hand, carefully surveyed the surrounding region. "Master, this is the western shore of the Heaven-Flowing River."

"This is too much," Tripitaka said. "The Guardians were told to take us straight to the Land of the East, so what do they mean by dropping us halfway home?"

"What's all the fuss?" Sandy asked. "The Master is no longer a mortal—we saw his body float by on that river—so we know he can't sink."

"You'll never get him across," Monkey said, for unlike the others, he knew that Tripitaka had not yet perfected the sacred number of nine times nine.

They began walking along the shore, discussing their plight, when suddenly they heard someone calling, "Priest of T'ang! Priest of T'ang! Come this way!" They looked all around but could not see where the voice was coming from, until at once they spotted a huge white turtle. Stretching its neck, it called out again, "My Master, I have been waiting for the longest time."

"Good turtle," Tripitaka said, "we meet again. You helped us cross this river once in the past, and now, if you will, you may help us cross it once again."

The turtle crawled up on the bank, and they all got on board, Monkey atop the horse, with Tripitaka and Sandy on each side. The turtle began to carry them across the river as if he were walking on dry land. "Steady as you go," Tripitaka said. "We are certainly in no hurry."

It was nearing dusk, and they were in sight of the other bank when the turtle spoke. "Old Master," he said, "the last time I took you across this river, I asked you to find out from Buddha when I would achieve human form. Did you remember to ask him?"

Tripitaka had been so preoccupied with his own problems and ordeals that he had completely forgotten his promise to the white turtle. Not wishing to lie, but afraid to tell the truth, he hemmed and hawed for as long as he could. But he was unable to fool the turtle, who suddenly dove to the bottom of the river, leaving the pilgrims to flounder in the river. Fortunately, the horse was really a dragon, and Pigsy and Sandy were both at home in the water, but only Monkey—displaying again his magic powers—was able to rescue Tripitaka and get him safely ashore. However, all of their luggage, including the scriptures, had gotten thoroughly soaked.

Once they were on the bank they began looking through the scriptures to see if any of the scrolls had received permanent damage. Suddenly some fishermen who were walking along the shore called out to them, "Are you not the reverend monks who had gone to India to seek scriptures? We see that all of your belongings have gotten wet. What has happened to you?"

After Tripitaka explained to them about their failed promise to the white turtle, they insisted that the pilgrims come home with them, dry their belongings, and have some food. Tripitaka was feeling desperate and was therefore happy to accept their invitation, as he could see that they were simple, honest people.

After they collected their scriptures, none of which had been seriously damaged, they set out for the fishermen's village. The news of their arrival had preceded them, and by the time they reached the gates of the city an incense stand had already been set up. Music could be heard in the streets, and the order had been given for a feast to be arranged in honor of the scripture-bearing priests.

When it came time for the feast, Tripitaka realized that because he had lost his mortal body he had little taste for earthly food. It was only out of politeness that he was able to make a show of tasting the various dishes that were put before him. Monkey, who rarely ate cooked food, was quickly sated, and like Monkey, Sandy too was soon satisfied. Even Pigsy did not eat with his usual gusto.

"What's the matter?" Monkey asked, looking over at Pigsy.

"I don't know what it is," Pigsy answered. "My stomach seems to have lost control of my mouth."

The tables were soon cleared, and the elders of the village insisted on a thorough account from Tripitaka on the trials they had endured in order to acquire the holy scriptures. "We can think of no better way to show our honor, respect, and gratitude to the pilgrims, than by establishing a shrine, to be called Life-Perpetuating Temple, that we might continually burn incense in your honor."

"Such blessings come from Heaven," Monkey said, "not from us. However, after we leave, we will provide what protection we can that all of the families of this village may enjoy abundance and prosperity, your herds multiply, and the winds and rains come in their season." The people all kowtowed, and immediately new offerings of fruit and cake were brought in. "It's just my luck," Pigsy giggled. "In the past no household would feed me, and today one family after another insists on bringing me food. I suppose I shouldn't be rude." So saying, he proceeded to eat nine dishes of vegetarian food and between twenty and thirty pastries. The food was still pouring in when Tripitaka begged of their hosts that they be allowed to take their leave. "It has grown very late," he said, "and tomorrow is another day."

That night Tripitaka did not sleep but kept guard over the scriptures. At the third watch he whispered to Monkey, "These people realize that we have mastered the secrets of the Way. It is said, 'The adept does not reveal himself; he who reveals himself is no adept.' I fear that they will detain us for as long as they can in order to fish out our secrets. We had better get out of here while it is still dark."

They wakened the others and set about loading their packs and arranging the luggage. Then they crept along in silence until they reached the main gate. It was locked, as Monkey had suspected it would be, but using his magic he quickly opened it, and they were soon traveling once again toward the Land of the East.

They had not gone far when they heard the voices of the Vajrapanis, crying from the air, "Come! Follow us!" A great gust of air, bearing a strange perfume, carried them up to the clouds.

The Western Paradise

*I*T took less than a day for the magic wind to blow the four pilgrims back to China. While the Vajrapanis waited in midair, Tripitaka and his disciples descended before the gates of the city, beside the Scripture Anticipation Tower. As soon as the Emperor and his officials saw Tripitaka, they came down from the tower to receive them. "Has our brother returned to us at last?" the Emperor asked. Tripitaka prostrated himself before the Emperor. "Who are these others?" the Emperor asked.

"These are the disciples I picked up along the way," Tripitaka replied. The Emperor greeted them and then called to one of his servants, "Have one of the chariot horses saddled so that Tripitaka can ride back to Court with me; the others can wait here."

When they reached the Audience Hall, the Emperor seated Tripitaka at his side and ordered the scriptures to be brought in. The scriptures had been delivered over to the chamberlains, who now brought them in and placed them before the Emperor. The Emperor was highly pleased and ordered a banquet to be prepared in the eastern tower. When he had issued his command he glanced up and noticed the three disciples standing off to one side at the end of the hall. Disturbed by their strange appearance, he turned to Tripitaka and said, "I take it these pilgrims are foreigners." Tripitaka nodded and smiled as he began to give the Emperor a full account of their origins and the invaluable service they had rendered during the pilgrimage to India.

The Emperor said, "Tell me, are your disciples familiar with Court etiquette?"

"I'm afraid not," Tripitaka said. "My disciples have known only the wilds and the life of mountain villages. I must ask your Majesty to make certain allowances."

"You needn't worry. We won't find fault with them, and they are certainly welcome." Tripitaka thanked the Emperor and called for his three disciples to join him.

The pilgrims were soon seated together with various officials, both civil and military, on both sides of the Emperor. Soon singing and dancing proceeded in a solemn and orderly manner. It was truly a magnificent day, and Tripitaka was impressed by the conduct of his disciples. Pigsy kept his voice down and did not make a scene over the food, and Monkey and Sandy behaved with perfect decorum. Tripitaka realized that their quiet reserve was the result of their illumination.

Early the next morning the Emperor held court and sent for Tripitaka. When all the ministers had been assembled, he addressed the priest. "I was unable to sleep this night, so full were my thoughts of the magnitude of our brother's achievement and the impossibility of our ever making adequate recompense for what you have brought us. We can think of nothing more fitting than to have our brother recite some of the scriptures, that we may hear them for the first time from his lips."

Tripitaka agreed, but said, "To read these scriptures aloud, a proper site must be found. The treasure palace is no place for recitations." The Emperor was impressed by the truth of Tripitaka's statement. Turning to his attendants, he asked, "Which is the holiest of temples in China?" The Grand

*At the end of his journey, Monkey reads
the sacred scriptures.*

Preceptor stepped forward and said, "The Wild Goose Pagoda is the holiest of all." The Emperor at once commanded that a few scrolls from the main scriptures be reverently carried to the designated pagoda.

A lofty platform was erected and seating appointments made. Tripitaka told Pigsy and Sandy to hold the dragon horse and mind the luggage, and for Monkey to arrange the scriptures and hand them to him when the time came for the recitation. While these arrangements were being made, Tripitaka turned to the Emperor and said, "My Lord, if these scriptures are to be circulated throughout the empire, we should take the precaution of making copies, for the originals should be treasured and handled lightly."

"The words of our brother are wisely spoken," the Emperor said. He immediately ordered the officials of Han-lin Academy and the Central Drafting Office to make copies of the scriptures.

Tripitaka mounted the platform and was about to begin his recitation when a gust of wind sent a strangely familiar perfume to his nostrils. Suddenly the eight Vajrapanis appeared in midair and spoke. "Recitants, forego your scriptures and follow us to the West." Immediately the pilgrims and their white horse ascended from the platform and joined the Vajrapanis. Startled and in utter amazement at what they had witnessed, the Emperor and all his ministers bowed down in homage.

When the Emperor and his court had finished their worship they began selecting a group of high priests for the next stage in their work. It wasn't long before a Grand Ceremony was held in the Wild Goose Pagoda and the true scriptures were read for the first time, with the result that a multitude of lost souls were saved from darkness and the true teaching was promulgated throughout the empire.

The pilgrims and their white horse were carried back to Paradise, the round trip having taken precisely eight days. Their arrival coincided with a lecture the Buddha was giving to an assembly of deities. The Vajrapanis ushered the Master and his disciples before the Buddha, declaring, "We have escorted your pilgrims back to China, where the scriptures were delivered, and we now return with them and surrender our decree." Tripitaka and his disciples were then motioned forward to the throne of Buddha to receive their Heavenly ranks.

Tripitaka was the first to be called. "Sage monk," the Buddha said, "in your previous incarnation you were my second disciple and were called Golden Cicada. Because you did not heed my teaching and belittled my doctrine, I caused you to be exiled to the East. By fetching the scriptures you have shown true faith and have won great merit. I hereby appoint you a buddha, with the title 'Buddha of Precocious Merit.'

"Monkey, because you caused great trouble in Heaven, I had to imprison you within the Mountain of Five Elements. Fortunately, when your incarceration ended you embraced the Great Teaching. By devoting yourself to the scourging of evil and the promotion of good you have earned your merit. Throughout the journey you subjugated monsters and demons, and defeated fiends with single-minded purpose. I now promote you to be the Buddha Victorious in Strife.

"Pigsy, you were originally a water marshal of the Heavenly River. When you got drunk at the Festival of Immortal Peaches and took liberties with a fairy maiden, you were banished to the Region Below and placed in the body of a beast. Although you continued to sin, you were eventually converted and embraced our vows. Greed and lust were never completely extinguished in you, but you protected the sage monk and toted the luggage during the entire journey. I therefore grant you a promotion and appoint you Cleanser of Altars."

"Hey! Wait a minute!" Pigsy exclaimed. "You made the others buddhas. What about me?"

"You are still too talkative and lazy, and your appetite is still too big. Within the four great continents my worshipers are many. It will be your job to clean up the altars after every ceremony and whenever offerings are made. There will be plenty to eat, so you have nothing to complain about.

"Sandy, you were originally the Curtain-Raising Captain, until you broke a crystal cup during the Festival of Immortal Peaches and were banished to the Lower Regions. Settling in the River of Flowing Sands, you sinned by devouring human flesh. Fortunately, you were converted to our faith and were zealous in your vows to protect the sage monk. You earned great merit by leading his horse over all the mountain passes. I now promote you to the rank of an arhat, with the title Golden-Bodied Arhat."

Buddha now turned to the dragon horse. "You were originally a prince, a child of the Dragon King of the Western Ocean, but you disobeyed your father and were found guilty of unfilial conduct. Fortunately, you submitted to the Law and were converted to our faith. Because you carried the sage monk to the West and also transported the scriptures back to the East, you too have earned great merit. I hereby promote you to be one of the eight Heavenly Dragons."

The four pilgrims and the white horse all kowtowed their thanks. The Buddha then ordered the white horse to be led to the Dragon Transforming Pool on Holy Mountain. After the white horse was pushed into the pool, he stretched himself and his coat began to shed, horns appeared on his head, and golden scales began to gleam from his body, while silver whiskers appeared on his cheeks. His whole body was immersed in an auspicious air of gold, and his four paws were shrouded in hallowed clouds. He soared up out of the pool and circled the monastery gate above the Pillars that Support Heaven. All the deities were overcome by the wonder of the miracle that Buddha had wrought, and they burst into exclamations of joy.

The pilgrims had become saints, and their promotion had taken place in the presence of all the spirits of Heaven. Now, when they took their appointed places in the great assembly, a voice rose in prayer and resounded throughout the temple, while the names of all the deities were chanted in accordance. At the very end of the ceremony were heard these words: "Praise to the Buddha of Precocious Merit, praise to the Buddha Victorious in Strife, praise to the Cleanser of Altars, praise to the Golden-Bodied Arhat, praise to the Heavenly Dragon."